How to get your lawn & garden

Pesticide-free gardening for a healthier environment.

& garden off drugs

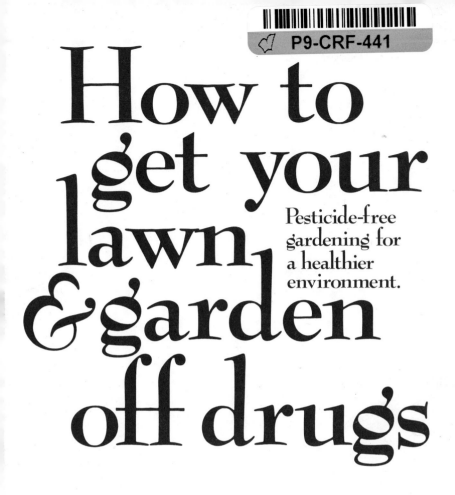

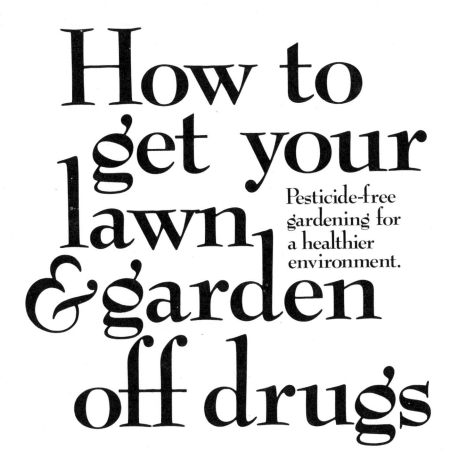

How to get your lawn & garden off drugs

Pesticide-free gardening for a healthier environment.

Carole Rubin

Friends of the Earth

Edited by Clifford Maynes
Cover design and illustrations by Joanne Purich
Third Printing, Whitecap edition

Typesetting and production by CristinArt

Printed and bound in Canada by D.W. Friesen and Sons Ltd.

Canadian Cataloguing in Publication Data.

Rubin, Carole.
   How to get your lawn & garden off drugs

   Includes index.
   ISBN 1-895099-84-6

   1. Organic gardening. 2. Lawns. 3. Landscape gardening.
4. Garden pests—Control. I.
Friends of the Earth (Canada). II. Title.
SB453.5.R82 1991   635.9'87   C91-091258-0

CONTENTS:

ACKNOWLEDGMENTS:

This book would not have been possible without the energetic support of Julia Langer, Executive Director, Friends of the Earth, Canada. Above and beyond the call kudos to editor Clifford Maynes, design team Joanne Purich and Alan Todd, and promotion coordinator, Ellie Barrington.

Thanks to Doctors Stuart Hill and Rod MacRae, MacDonald College, McGill University, Quebec; Ron Labonté, Department of Health, Toronto; Ivy Wile, Ministry of Environment, Ontario; The Canadian Organic Growers Association; the Bio-Integral Resources Centre, Berkeley, California; and the National Coalition Against the Misuse of Pesticides, Washington, D.C. for technical support.

I also want to thank all the organic farmers and gardeners across Canada who shared their wisdom with the stranger on the other end of the telephone. May this volume help to spread our vision.

HOW TO USE THIS BOOK:

The Chapters on lawns, gardens and landscaping have been designed to stand alone. However, all depend on a thorough grounding in the principles of soil preparation outlined in Chapter 2.

• If you are a relative newcomer to the world of organic gardening techniques, we suggest that you start by reading through the entire book to gain a general feel for this approach, before implementing the measures described in each chapter.

• There are Troubleshooting sections in Chapters 3, 4 and 5, outlining least-toxic treatments if pests do become a problem. If you run across terms you don't understand, check the Glossary in the back of the book.

• You will also find a sample listing of Suppliers in each province who carry the products recommended in these pages, as well as a directory of Soil Testing and Pest Identification Labs across Canada. Finally, a Further Reading section provides a sampling of specialized reference material for your information.

PREFACE:

Silent Spring: The title of Rachel Carson's pace-setting book on planetary pesticide contamination is enough to send chills down the spine. In 1962 she portrayed the ecologically disastrous consequences of pesticide use (or rather abuse), using DDT as a prime example. While a few measures to avert the truly catastrophic consequences have been taken in North America and Europe, the massive applications of pesticides to agricultural, forest and urban lands is taking its toll. The warnings seem to have been falling on deaf ears and the costs are adding up.

The earth's soil has been chemically driven into intense production. Now depleted and eroded, the soil is being artificially boosted in a vicious cycle of chemical subsidy in order to feed us. This cannot continue forever.

The impact on human health can be fatal. The World Health Organization estimates over 20,000 deaths yearly, mostly in the Third World where dangerous pesticides, many of them banned from use in North America, are used uncontrolled. Poisoning, birth defects and other illness from exposure to pesticides are not uncommon. And it doesn't stop there. Pesticides banned or restricted here but used on food crops far away come back to us on our food completing a dangerous 'circle of poison'.

Pesticides and chemical fertilizers have been responsible for the near collapse of entire species, sensitive to their various toxic effects. No ecosystem or organism is safe or unaffected. Pesticides are found in the bodies of polar bears far from any direct source, in the water and fish of remote lakes, and in every person on earth.

FRIENDS OF THE EARTH
701-251 Laurier Ave. W.
Ottawa, Ontario K1P 5J6
Canada

This litany of insults has been substantiated by scientific data.

Still, massive pesticide and artificial chemical application continues, in spite of the contradictory and counter-productive results. Where is the logic in using chemicals to pump up depleted soils to produce food when this further depletes the soils? Is it right to spray forests when fish and birds will suffer? How can we justify using chemicals to make parks green when children are going to play on the grass? What is the sense of using toxic chemicals to produce food which is supposed to keep us nourished and healthy?

The point is not to stop producing food or tending our lawns, but to do it in a healthy and sustainable way. Alternatives are available. They will take some foresight, energy and creativity to implement, but we think this is the only option. Urban lawns and gardens are a small but significant microcosm of the pesticide problem. Acre for acre, approximately 15 times more pesticides are applied on cities than rural areas, and the opportunities for passer-by exposure is high.

We offer an alternative with this book. Our lawn and garden care program is easy, convenient and effective. It can be applied to all tended urban landscaping. By rejecting artificial chemical pesticides and fertilizers, individuals, communities, consumers, and voters can send a very clear message about chemical use in other areas. We can and must break from chemical dependency, to create a healthier, sustainable environment.

Julia Langer, Executive Director,
Friends of the Earth, May, 1989

CHAPTER 1:

INTRODUCTION TO THE ORGANIC APPROACH

Since the Second World War, chemical fertilizers and pesticides have been promoted as the technological cure-all for soil nutrition and the "management" of plant insects, weeds, and diseases.

Today, after 40 years of chemical gardening, we are looking for ways to clean these agrochemicals from our water, fisheries, wildlife species, soils—and our bodies. And we are looking for ways to reverse damage to soils which have been depleted of organic material and sometimes reduced to a sterile, toxic sand as a result of repeated chemical treatments.

CHEMICAL FERTILIZERS:
The not-so-healthy quick fix

Fast-releasing chemical fertilizers send a rush of nitrogen to the soil. But in order to make use of the nutrients in this fertilizer, the soil microbes must take energy from organic matter. The organic matter is gradually depleted, and the soil becomes progressively more lifeless.

The less organic matter in the soil, the more fertilizer it needs to support plant life. A cycle of chemical dependency is established.

Furthermore, chemical nitrogen has short-lived benefits. It is highly water-soluble, and it quickly leaches away into the water tables under the soil. Organically poor soil speeds the leaching process.

Over-use of chemical fertilizers can also kill beneficial organisms in the soil, lowering your plants' defences against harmful insects and disease. Recent studies at Cornell University found fewer harmful insects on collards fertilized with manure than on those fertilized with synthetics.

Over-use of chemical fertilizers also disrupts the pH balance of your soil, making it acidic.

CHEMICAL PESTICIDES:
The toxic arsenal

Chemical pesticides were first formulated during the Second World War as agents of chemical warfare. Herbicides, insecticides, fungicides and other toxic agents have since been developed for use in agriculture and home gardening to kill unwanted weeds, insects, and diseases. The problem is, they don't know when to stop killing.

Today, many pesticides are considered to be carcinogenic (cancer- causing) in human beings. There is increasing concern about pesticide residues on food.

Chemical pesticides run off into the surrounding soils and water systems, remaining in their toxic state, or breaking down into substances that are sometimes even

Synthetic chemical pesticides (including fungicides, insecticides, and herbicides) were first manufactured as agents of chemical warfare. Many that are in use today are considered to be carcinogenic to humans and other species. While they are registered for use by Agriculture Canada, Health and Welfare Canada has stated that registration is not a guarantee of safety.

more harmful to the environment.

Pesticides also kill beneficial insects and soil micro-organisms that act as natural predators of plant pests. Pests soon reassert themselves, but this time around the problem is worse because the "good bugs" are no longer there to help maintain a balance in your garden's ecosystem. More pesticides are needed. Once again, a cycle of chemical dependency is established.

ALTERNATIVES TO SYNTHETICS:
Organic Care

Had enough? We hope so. Because lawns and gardens can flourish without the use of synthetic chemicals.

If you use balanced organic alternatives that nourish the soil and your crops, followed up with a proper maintenance programme, you can have the satisfaction of beautiful plants and safe vegetables in a healthy environment you helped to create.

The organic approach described in this book consists of six basic principles, outlined in more detail in the following chapters:

1. SOIL PREPARATION:
An organically fed soil
is a happy soil

Healthy, pest-resistant plants depend on healthy soil. Your soil needs a regular diet of organic amendments (additions). Unlike synthetic fertilizers, these amendments are slow-releasing, long- lasting, harmless to healthy soil microbes, and closely matched to the soil's own structure.

2. PLANT SELECTION:
Why magnolias do poorly in Sudbury

If the rose bush your aunt gave you is covered in blight, maybe it is the wrong plant for your growing conditions. Many gardening problems can be eliminated by growing pest-resistant and disease- resistant plants that are suited to your climate and soil type.

3. TOLERANCE LEVELS:
Or how to make friends with a Buttercup

Canadians have a strange obsession about pests, far out of proportion to the damage they cause. Only one per cent of insects actually harm plants. If you rethink your tolerance levels, you can often find a happy balance between your own needs and the competitive demands of other species. Are those buttercups too much to tolerate, or are they part of a beautiful yard?

4. PROPER MAINTENANCE:
Not too much, not too little

Both neglect and excessive attention can put your plants under stress, attracting pests. You need to find a happy medium.

5. MONITORING:
Getting to know your grounds, intimately

If you monitor your grounds and gardens regularly you will spot problems at an early stage. You can then limit the damage and reduce the need for drastic remedies.

6. LEAST-TOXIC PEST MANAGEMENT:
When all else fails . . .

When preventive measures are inadequate, you can adopt a least- toxic treatment strategy. Each chapter in this booklet provides advice for organic troubleshooting.

These basic steps, and the programme outlined in the following chapters, will provide you with healthy soils and plants maintained in a way which respects and assists the balance of nature. Instead of keeping your family off the grounds and fearing to eat your home-grown vegetables after a chemical application, you'll be able to join the birds, ladybugs, earthworms, and occasional dandelion in your organic yard—in an environment that is healthy and safe.

CHAPTER 2:

SOIL: LAYING
THE GROUND-WORK

Successful lawns, gardens, and land-scaping depends on healthy "topsoil" – the 15 cm (6 inch) layer of earth which sustains all plant life. Neglected or chemically abused soil probably suffers from all or some of the following maladies:

- Poor air circulation.
- Poor (excessive or inadequate) drainage.
- Inadequate or imbalanced nutrient content.
- Inappropriate pH (acidity).
- The absence of helpful worms, bugs, bacteria, and other soil life which are needed to break up the earth and make nutrients available for use by plants.

Unhealthy soil produces weak vegetation which is vulnerable to pests and diseases and unable to compete with weeds.

This chapter outlines a programme which will help you wean your soil from chemical dependency and maintain a nutritious and well balanced medium for your plants. Healthy soil breeds healthy plants. And healthy plants, as we have said, can fend off weeds, pests and diseases without chemical treatments. When pests become a problem, relatively non-toxic remedies are available, listed in the Troubleshooting

A SPECIAL NOTE:
For those moving into newly-built homes: Building contractors usually remove most of the topsoil, leaving only a thin, inadequate layer of sub-soil as a base for seed or sod. Make sure your building contractor leaves 15 cm (6 inches) of topsoil at the lawn site. Otherwise, it may be scraped off, sold to a nursery, and sold back to you.

sections of the next three chapters on Lawns, Gardens, and Landscaping.

Soil TESTING:

It's a good idea to have your soil tested for pH balance, nitrogen, phosphorus, potassium, sulphur, calcium and magnesium content. Sending a soil sample to a

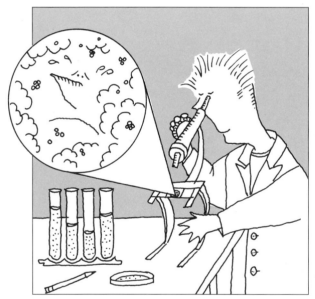

professional organic lab is well worth the extra time and small financial investment. Your results will tell you exactly how much of each organic amendment to add to your lawn or garden.

SOIL TESTING:
Determining the deficits

It's a pretty good bet that your soil is generally nutrient- deficient, especially if it has been abused or neglected. It will likely need topping up with organic amendments to balance the pH and correct for nutrient deficiencies. Without these additions your soil will continue to produce weak and vulnerable plants.

Many organic gardeners have their soil tested to identify pH balance (acidity) as well as deficiencies and excesses of specific nutrients. This allows them to correct the imbalances using the organic amendments listed below.

Home testing kits are available at most garden supply centres. They are fast, but they provide very limited information. Professional soil-testing laboratories take more time, but they can provide much more detailed information and are well worth the wait.

If possible, choose a laboratory which provides organic results (see Soil Testing and Pest Identification Labs). An organic analysis will tell you exactly how much of each amendment your soil needs for the correct pH and nutrient balance.

Unfortunately, many of labs listed in the Sources section do not provide organic results. Their results are geared to the use of prepared mixtures of chemical fertilizers. Other labs provide organic results some of the time, but only on request. Be sure to ask.

Get your soil tested in early spring, before you dig your beds. Then add any fertilizers, compost or manure. You need to test only once every three to five years.

Contact the lab beforehand for information about fees, preparation and shipping of samples, and response time for results. An organic analysis generally costs from $15 to $30, while a conventional analysis costs from nothing to $15, depending on the tests requested. The first time, we recommend that you have your soil tested for nitrogen, phosphorus, potassium, sulphur, calcium, and magnesium as well as pH. On subsequent occasions, nitrogen, phosphorus, potassium and pH are probably adequate.

THE pH FACTOR:
Sweet or sour?

Your soil needs to be the correct pH for the plants you are growing as acidity affects the availability of nutrients to your plants.

The following amendments are available for adjusting soil pH. (See the Suppliers section in the back of this book for sources of all organic amendments.) Add only in the amounts recommended by your test results, as over-liming can seriously damage the pH balance of your soil.

- Dolomitic lime (high magnesium). Use to increase alkalinity where soil needs

ABOUT pH:

On a 14-point scale, pH of 7 is neutral, less than 7 is acid, and greater than 7 is alkaline. The majority of grasses, plants and shrubs enjoy a slightly acid pH of 6.5, which is usually considered "normal" in gardening. However, some plants have special requirements for acidic soil (below pH 6.5) or more alkaline soil (pH 7.0 or higher). For information about specific plants, check gardening reference books or with the nursery where you buy your plants.

magnesium as well as calcium.

- Hi-cal lime (high in calcium). Use to increase alkalinity where soil has adequate or excessive magnesium
- Flowers of sulphur. Use to increase soil acidity.

Apply lime or flowers of sulphur as required in fall or spring, well in advance of the planting season (see Digging, below). Spread evenly and thoroughly, and wear a mask or kerchief and gloves. Mix into the top 15 cm (six inches) of soil.

ORGANIC FERTILIZERS:
Feed a soil, starve a pest

Healthy soil contains a variety of nutrients which are gradually released into the soil as organic material decomposes. The three main nutrients required are nitrogen (N), phosphorus (P), and potassium (K). Fertilizers are usually identified according to their percentage content of each of these three. For example, (21 - 7 - 7) fertilizer contains 21 per cent nitrogen, 7 per cent phosphorus, and 7 per cent potassium.

In addition, soil requires other "macronutrients" including sulphur, calcium, and magnesium, and several "micronutrients" or "trace elements" such as iron, boron, and zinc.

The following amendments are recommended for balancing the nutrients in your soil's diet. Add only in the amounts recommended by your soil test results, as over-amending can disrupt the soil's ecosystem. Don't exceed the annual maximum dose.

In the following listings, the bracketed numbers - for example, (6-2-1) - stand for the percentage of nitrogen, phosphorous,

FERTILIZER BLENDS: Pre-mixed organic fertilizer blends can't always be depended upon, as your soil's requirements may not match the ratios of ingredients in a manufactured blend. You should purchase and apply the particular nutrients that your soil needs in the proper amounts, as indicated on your test resutls. This will ensure balanced feeding.

and potassium respectively contained in the fertilizer. Maximum application rates for each year are given in metric and imperial measurements, followed by the length of time the treatment should last.

Fall applications are best for established lawns, spring for gardens and new lawn beds. Make sure to apply at least six to eight weeks before planting. Mix the fertilizers into the top 10 to 15 cm (4 to 6 inches) of your topsoil. If your lawn or plants are already established, apply as a top-dressing or side-dressing, especially after aerating.(see Chapter 3 and Glossary)

Cover your mouth and nose with kerchief or mask. If you are making a blend, mix it in a large dry container such as a plastic bucket with a wooden spoon. Wear gloves.

Carry small quantities of fertilizer in a plastic juice pitcher. Carry large quantities in a wheelbarrow or spreader, and apply evenly.

ORGANIC NITROGEN SOURCES:

Canola seed meal: (6-2-1). Maximum 5 kilograms/10 square metres (10 lb./100 square feet). Lasts five months.

Fish meal: (10.5-6-0). Maximum 2.5 kilograms/10 square metres (5 lb./100 square feet). Lasts six to eight months.

Blood meal: (12.5-1-3). Maximum 1.5 kilograms/10 square metres (3 lb/100 square feet). Lasts four months.

Hoof and horn meal: (14-2-0). Maximum 2 kilograms/10 square metres (4 lb/100 square feet). Starts releasing in four to six weeks, and lasts 12 months.

When to Feed:

Add organic fertilizers to freshly-dug garden or new lawn beds in early spring (see the section on Digging). If your lawn is already established, add fertilizers in the fall. Be sure to spread these nutrients evenly over the beds: avoid feeding in patches!

ORGANIC PHOSPHOROUS SOURCES:

Bone meal: (3-20-0) plus 20 to 30 per cent calcium. Maximum 2.5 kilograms/10 square metres (5 lb/100 square feet). Lasts more than 12 months.

Single Super Phosphate: (0-20-0) plus 20 per cent calcium and 12 per cent sulphur. Maximum 2.5 kilograms/10 square metres (5lb/100 square feet). Starts release in two to three months.

ORGANIC POTASSIUM SOURCES:

Kelp meal and liquid seaweed: (1-0-1.2) plus 33 per cent trace minerals. Maximum 0.5 kilogram/10 square metres (1 lb/100 square feet). Lasts six to 12 months.

Wood ashes: (0-0-1) to (0-0-10). Variable nutrient levels. Ashes of hardwoods are best. Raises soil pH too. Maximum 1 kilogram/10 square metres (2 lb/100 square feet). Lasts more than 12 months.

MISCELLANEOUS NATURAL AMENDMENTS:

Calcium sulphate: 23 to 57 per cent calcium, 17.7 per cent sulphur. Use where magnesium needs to be reduced, and calcium added, but where pH levels are already adequate or even too high. Use only according to soil test results: from 0.5 to 5 kilograms/10 square metres (from 1 to 10 lb/100 square feet).

Sulphate of potash magnesia (Sulpomag): (0-0-22) plus 11 per cent magnesium and 22 per cent sulphur. Use where calcium is plentiful, and magnesium and potash are deficient.

Leonardite and other mixtures: approximately 15 per cent humic materials and 15 per cent humic acid. A source of

THE RADIOACTIVITY FACTOR: ROCK PHOSPHATE

The phosphate in Single Super Phosphate is from Israel or North Africa, and is therefore not radioactive. We have not recommended rock phosphates as they usually come from North American mines that are high in uranium content. Greensand, a potassium source, is also high in uranium, and has been left off our list.

concentrated humates and humic acids that help make nutrients available to plants and lawns. Apply in fall, or at least a month before compost is added.

Fertilizer blends: Some companies offer personally designed blends made from rock powders, compost, and other natural products. Some have been designed to nourish specific plants, while other blends have been manufactured for all-purpose uses. As mentioned earlier, all purpose blends may not match your soil's needs. Be sure you need what the blend is offering before you buy.

Sulphate of potash: (0-0-50) plus 18 per cent sulphur. Use where potash is deficient.

COMPOST:
That 'Old Black Magic'

All soils benefit from nutrient-rich applications of compost at any time. Compost, made from rotted organic matter, is the best all-around soil conditioner available to the gardener. It improves the physical and biological condition of the soil by providing beneficial micro-organisms, excellent drainage, and both the major and minor plant nutrients. Could you ask for more?

Compost can be added to soil throughout the season. It is almost impossible to use too much.

Start digging it into your topsoil as soon as the soil is warm and dry enough to work in spring (see Digging, page 26). If the soil is soggy, it's too soon. Compost should also be added to growing gardens, lawns, and trees as a top-dressing or side-dressing throughout the growing season. Before application to lawns, sift the compost through a screen (see Suppliers) and apply only the finer-grained material.

Compost can be made in perforated garbage cans, cylinders made from chicken wire, or bins created by stacking cement blocks. For no-fuss no-muss compost in small amounts, use a garbage bag. Compost made in plastic bags will be more

HOW TO MAKE COMPOST:

Commercial compost mixes are available in garden supply centres, but making your own is inexpensive and easy. It also helps to reduce the volume of municipal waste going to landfill sites.

Use kitchen scraps, grass clippings (if not infested or recently sprayed with an herbicide), fallen leaves (avoid walnut tree leaves and all droppings from conifers), livestock manures, spoiled hay, and straw. Avoid meat or bone scraps, which attract animals.

Two recipes for compost are described below. Compost is ready to use when it is cool, and fairly dark and crumbly. Some shape of the original organic matter should still be evident.

BAG–IT: The Hassle-Free Recipe for City Dwellers

City gardeners can avoid smell

moist than outdoor piles. Try to add coffee grounds and a few cupfuls of topsoil to your shredded scraps in the bag. After two weeks in a sunny ➡

and unsightliness by putting small scraps of kitchen garbage (fruit peels, egg shells, vegetable leftovers, coffee grounds and used tea-bags, etc.) into a black plastic garbage bag. Tie the bag and place it in a sunny spot outdoors.

Composting should be complete in two to three weeks. For faster compost, cut the scraps into small pieces before bagging.

THE MECHANICS OF THE OUTDOOR COMPOST PILE:

Larger amounts of compost can be prepared inoffensively in a compost container or bin (see recipe below). If possible, locate the pile at the edge of your garden in full sun. The pile should be exposed to the air on all sides. Use a perforated garbage can, cylinders made from chicken wire or snow fencing, or a four foot square cement block bin, open on one side for easy access.

To eliminate most odours and achieve a higher rate of decomposition, turn the pile occasionally to keep it well aerated. When the pile has shrunken in size, you know it's "working". Use a pitch fork or shovel to turn material over. Turning frequency depends on how fast the pile is working. Cover the pile with a sheet of clear plastic to speed decomposition.

THE 14-DAY OUTDOOR COMPOST RECIPE:

A summer pile can be composted in two weeks if the ingredients are shredded. Use a power shredder, or cut-as-you-go in the kitchen. Layer materials in your bin as follows:

- 2.5 cm (one-inch) base layer of brush on bottom, such as grass clippings, straw or ruined hay,

- 15 cm (six inches) of "green matter" such as kitchen peels, egg shells, coffee grounds, ruined hay, and leaves,

- 5 cm (two inches) of manure, sterilized, if possible

- a sprinkling of topsoil and limestone.

spot, empty the contents of the bag in a corner of your backyard. Dig in some more topsoil, turn it over, and let the pile continue to work for a few days before adding to your garden. If you intend to use the compost on your lawn, it should be fairly dry and screened first.

Repeat the layers until the pile reaches at least 1 metre (3 feet) high. Turn the moistened pile on the fourth, seventh and tenth days, after at least a cubic metre (a cubic yard) of material has been collected and shredded. Presto: black magic!

ROTTED MANURE:
The true meaning of recycling

Rotted or composted manure is another balanced source of available nutrients for your soil. Manure is widely available in bags for home use in supermarkets and garden centres. Manure in this form has generally been sterilized, which means that weed seeds have been killed. If you buy manure from a farmer there is always the danger that is has not been adequately rotted, and that it will introduce weeds into your garden.

Dig in about 50 kilograms/10 square metres (100 pounds/100 square feet) in your garden each spring, taking care to dig it in below the 15 cm (6 inch) level (see Digging, below).

CONDITIONING AND AMENDING:
Dig, dig, dig!

If you are starting a new garden or lawn, examine the soil carefully. If it is lifeless clay or sand, it is probably beyond repair. The topsoil may have been removed entirely. The only solution is to truck in enough new topsoil to create a 15 cm (6 inch) base layer. Have it tested for pH and nutrients, and add the required amendments recommended above.

If the soil is brown, however, and appears to have some organic content, it can be brought back to health. Digging is essential for conditioned soil because it:

- Allows roots to reach deep and grow unimpeded by stones, clumps of hard earth, and old organic matter.

- Helps to create good drainage and air circulation in the soil.

- Works compost and other organic amendments into the soil.

- Discourages harmful root-feeding insects which will leave once the soil is worked and the old roots they feed on are removed.

Dig all soils after sending out your soil sample to a lab and before planting. Dig garden beds twice a year, in spring and fall. Start in spring as soon as the earth has lost that sodden quality (about one or two months before planting). Get in there with shovel and hoe, and turn the soil over to a depth of about 15 cm (six inches). Pile the soil alongside the area you are working, and break up the bottom of your trench with a spade. Watch for underground cables.

This is the perfect time to add rotted manure. Mix manure with the broken earth in the bottom of the trench and with the topsoil.

This is also the perfect time to add soil amendments such as compost, lime or sulphur, and the other organic fertilizers listed above. If soil contains excessive clay and drainage is poor, add some sand. If it is too sandy, add some topsoil or peat moss.

Replace the topsoil, working in these amendments at the 10 to 15 cm (4 to 6 inch) level. Make sure that all stones, trash, and weed roots have been removed.

Gardeners should mound the soil into

Digging is the first rite of spring for many gardeners. It's the time to add fertilizers, lime, compost and rotted manure to new lawn and garden beds. You can start as soon as the earth has lost it's winter sogginess. Make sure to send your soil sample off to a lab before you dig or add any nutrients!

raised rows or beds in preparation for planting (see Chapter 4).

Now that you've prepared a soil base that is well cultivated, rich in organic matter, pH balanced and fed, you're ready (weather permitting) to plant.

CHAPTER 3:

THE CHEMICAL-FREE LAWN

This chapter tells you how to select, monitor, water, mow, feed, aerate, and generally maintain your lawn without chemical fertilizer and pesticides. If you follow these steps, you will have a healthy lawn that optimizes growth of grasses and minimizes opportunities for pest insects, weeds, or diseases.

Remedies for specific pests can be found in the Troubleshooting section at the end of this chapter.

A word about lawn-care and landscaping contractors: a recent survey in Montreal's west end showed customers of lawn-care services were unaware that chemical pesticides were routinely used on their premises. Ask your service for details about its methods. Advocate a switch to the non-chemical maintenance programme outlined in this book. If your company is reluctant to switch to organics, look around for another, or hire an individual who will maintain your lawn organically.

Launching a full-scale toxic chemical attack to eradicate pests is not necessary or healthy. Very few weeds or insects actually harm your lawn.

Pesticides used by lawn-care services must be registered for use in Canada. However, registration means only that the product meets minimum government standards. It does not guarantee safety.

ESTABLISHING TOLERANCE LEVELS:
So what's wrong with a buttercup or two?

It's important to remember that all lawns harbour some pests, whether or not pesticides are used. The trick is to keep pest numbers low enough to prevent significant damage to the grass. What constitutes "significant damage", and more important, what constitutes a healthy lawn, is a very personal decision.

If you want your lawn to look like a perfect "green rug", you're probably better off with indoor-outdoor carpeting. Otherwise, you should be prepared to tolerate-and even enjoy-a few buttercups or primroses.

Very few weeds or insects actually harm your lawn. Some "weeds", like creeping charlie, are quite attractive. Others are beneficial. Clover provides grass with nitrogen. Cornflowers indicate soil acidity: when the blossoms are blue, soil is alkaline; when blossoms are pink, soil is acidic.

Tolerance also depends on use. If you use your lawn for a putting green, for example, your tolerance level for weeds will be much lower than if your children and pets use the yard to play in. So take some time to think about your priorities.

PLANTING OR UPGRADING YOUR LAWN:
Can you say "En-do-phy-tic?"

To minimize maintenance requirements, pests, and diseases, start off by choosing well-adapted and disease-resistant grass varieties.

If you are starting a new lawn, begin by following the advice about soil preparation in Chapter 2. Then seed with a mix of ryegrasses, fescue, and Kentucky Blue-grasses, which has been found to be the hardiest blend. Look for pre-mixed packages containing the appropriate varieties. Water generously and prevent foot traffic over the seeded area.

Check the listings on the next page for recommended grass varieties that should be included in your seed mix. Your local landscape contractor or garden supply centre salesperson will tell you which of these varieties are best suited to your particular location and climate.

Your existing lawn probably consists of mostly Bluegrass blends. To upgrade, add one of the recommended ryegrasses for a hardier, more pest-resistant lawn. Spread the seed when you aerate and top-dress with compost (see Aeration, below).

Some of the ryegrass varieties listed (marked 🍂) contain a naturally occurring fungus that actually resists disease and some common lawn pests such as sod webworms and army worms. This endo-phytic fungus lives in the leaves and stems of certain grasses, causing no harm to the host plant.

Ryegrass doesn't live as long as blue-grasses, so you'll have to keep adding it periodically to maintain a hardy mix. Add at least once a year by top-dressing when-ever you aerate.

SEED STORAGE:

Since the viability of the endophytic fungi is lost with storage longer than two years, make sure you get fresh seed. Store the seed in a cool dry place and use it within nine months of purchase.

RECOMMENDED GRASS VARIETIES

All of the following grasses are known for their hardiness. All have tested high for turf quality and resistance to brown blight disease, fusarium and brown patch. All do well in Canadian climates.

Pest-resistant Perennial Ryegrasses:

❧ Repell (GT II)	❧ Dasher
❧ Citation	❧ Prelude
❧ Gator	❧ Diplomat
❧ All Star	❧ Manhattan II
❧ Omega II	❧ Palmer
❧ Yorktown II	Pennant
Blazer	Barry
Fiesta	

Pest-resistant Tall Fescue:

Apache	Rebell II

Pest-resistant Kentucky Bluegrass:

Baron or ask your dealer for other suggestions.

THE MAINTENANCE REGIME:
Five Steps to a Beautiful Pest- Resistant Lawn

STEP ONE: Aeration
Take a deep breath

A major cause of weed problems in Canadian lawns is compaction of the soil immediately under the roots. Compacted soil stresses and kills the roots of your lawn grasses, allowing weeds to move in and take their place.

Fortunately, you can remedy soil compaction by aerating the soil as part of your regular maintenance programme, using a tool that cuts narrow plugs out of the sod. This allows oxygen to penetrate the soil, and restores proper drainage.

Many lawn care companies have abandoned aeration in favour of herbicide treatments. Herbicides are less labour-intensive but they are also more expensive. And they do not correct the cause of weed growth. The weeds will sprout again, inviting repeated herbicide applications.

Most lawns should be aerated at least twice a year, once in early spring and once in fall. This timetable avoids periods when problem weeds are germinating.

After spring aeration, top-dress with screened compost and pest-resistant grass varieties. Lime if necessary. Immediately after aerating in fall, fertilize as needed using the amendments suggested in the Chapter 2.

Mid-season aeration is recommended for lawns with heavy thatch, and for top-dressing sod with compost and pest-resistant ryegrasses.

You may want to get together with your neighbours and purchase or rent an aerating tool or machine. Hand-held, self-propelled, towable, and tractor-mounted models are available. Check with your local garden supply centre. One warning: Avoid underground cables.

After Spring aeration, spread screened compost and pest-resistant seed over your

lawn. Use the back of a rake to force the mixture into the holes, and then water. In the Fall, fertilize after aerating, using the amendments suggested in Chapter Two.

STEP TWO: De-thatching
Banish that thatch!

Thatch is a dense layer of dead grass stems and roots compacted on the surface of the soil. It is resistant to decay. A deep layer of thatch tends to prevent water from soaking into the soil beneath. Thus, the tops or "crowns" of grasses are too wet, while the roots are too dry.

A thatch layer of 3 to 12 millimetres (one-eighth to one-half inch) is tolerable. A thicker layer encourages insects and disease, and increases your lawn's susceptibility to cold, heat, and drought. If you notice an increase in insects and diseases, chances are you have a thick layer of thatch harbouring the pests.

If you discover thatch in late spring or summer, aerate your lawn as an interim measure and top-dress with screened compost.

In fall, de-thatch with a heavy thatch rake, made expressly for the purpose, or with a verti-cutter. De-thatching creates some stress for your lawn, but it is temporary. You can diminish the shock by top-dressing with compost.

Step Three: Fertilizers and pH
It is what it eats.

You already know all about pH balance, organic fertilizers and compost from reading Chapter 2. This is just a reminder to apply that knowledge - and the goods - to your lawn to ensure a proper nutrient balance.

Fertilize established lawns in the fall and add pH balancers in the spring, after aerating. Fertilize soil beds for new lawns during spring digging. Add finely-screened compost throughout the season by top-dressing after aeration.

De-Thatching:

In Fall, use a special de-thatching rake or a verti-cutter to de-thatch your lawn. Don't de-thatch in Spring or Summer. Instead aerate and top-dress with screened compost as an interim measure. Be sure to pick up your grass clippings when you mow to prevent new thatch build-up. If the clippings are disease and chemical-free, add them to your compost pile, or to a mulch mixture.

STEP FOUR: Watering
How much, how often?

Improper watering is another major cause of disease and insect problems in Canadian lawns. Each summer, neighbours watch neighbours watering their lawns through the day and evening, moving the sprinklers to a new spot every half hour.

This ritual does more harm than good. Frequent shallow watering promotes shallow roots, which reduces the ability of the lawn to resist stress. Water long enough to allow a deep soaking to the roots (usually about an hour). If your lawn is large, establish a watering rotation schedule, soaking sections each day.

At least one day after watering, use a screwdriver or sharpened wooden chopstick to probe the soil for root and moisture depth. The moisture mark on the probe should reach to root depth.

Timing is important. Don't water in the evenings: the sod will remain wet throughout the cool of the night, promoting fungus and disease. Don't water in the full hot summer sun: the water will evaporate, and the sun will burn the grass. Ideally, lawns should be watered in the early morning. This allows proper soaking-in time before the burning sun or night chill sets in.

Allow soil to become nearly dry between waterings. Again, use the test probe to check for moisture. Dry soil around roots inhibits weed seed germination and kills weed seedlings. Generally, this means watering less than once a week.

If puddles appear on your lawn, you need to de-thatch or aerate. If the sod is uneven, level it with topsoil to reduce water-logged low spots that promote weeds and diseases.

TO AVOID
SOGGY GRASS:

Water infrequently (once a week) in the mornings and enough that it penetrates right down to the bottom of your grass roots after each irrigation. The roots should be allowed to nearly dry before the next hosing session.

STEP FIVE: Mowing
The Brush-Cut Is Dead

Mowing your lawn may seem to be an obvious procedure, but it's astonishing how many disease and weed problems are directly attributable to improper mowing practices.

Most lawns are mowed too short and too often. If frequent and close mowing is combined with other stresses such as drought, insufficient nutrients, or unusually hot or cold spells, grass plants become smaller in size and less dense. Thinning provides openings for undesirable weed species.

THE BRUSH-CUT
IS DEAD:
**Most lawns are mowed
too short, too often.**

Continual cutting also creates wounds at the ends of grass blades, providing ports of entry for diseases such as leaf spot, rust, and dollar spot. In fact, at the U.S. Department of Agriculture's experimental lawn plots, it is standard practice to mow shorter and more often to incite lawn diseases for experiments.

Keep your mower blades sharp, and as high off the ground as possible. In the spring and fall, when most grasses are in growing spurts, set the blades at 6 to 7.5 cm (2.5 to 3 inches).

In the summer months, set the blades at 7.5 cm (3 inches) for most varieties, or 10 cm (four inches) if your lawn contains Canada Bluegrass. Always collect grass cuttings in a bag attachment to prevent weeds from reseeding.

Allow the grass to grow at least 2.5 cm (1 inch) above the mowing height before cutting it again. In general, cut once every seven to ten days. This gives grasses time to recover from the previous mowing, and to produce new blades of grass from the growing points. At the same time, it is sufficiently frequent to exhaust weed plants attempting to establish a home in your lawn.

In order to avoid compaction of the soil under your lawn, change your mowing patterns and points of entry to the lawn as often as possible. And if your cuttings are diseased, don't add them to your compost pile.

TIPS FOR TRANSITION:
How to get your lawn off drugs

If your lawn is currently managed with chemical fertilizers and pesticides, it needs a little extra help. Aerate three times a year, in early spring, mid-summer, and fall, and top-dress with pest-resistant seed and finely screened compost.

If your lawn is recent sod, aerate in spring and at least twice in summer. Top-dress immediately afterward with coarse sand (available at your nursery) and screened compost. Aerate again in fall and add fertilizers and pH balancers. Of course, the previous steps should be followed throughout the season to minimize weed, disease and pest problems.

Give a copy of this book to your land-scaping contractor to ensure a shared understanding about your new lawn maintenance programme.

TRANSITION TIP:

One way to help build up topsoil under laid sod is to aerate three times a year and then topdress with screened compost, endophytic rye seed and coarse sand. (available at your nursery).

A word of warning: if you simply leave your lawn on its own to go "cold turkey" from chemical treatment without extra help, it may not survive.

MONITORING FOR INSECTS:
Pest or guest - and
how to find out

Once each week, or before you mow, randomly select four lawn sites to sample. They can be 30 to 90 cm (1 to 3 feet) square, depending on the size of your lawn. One of the areas should be adjacent to a sidewalk or patio as cement causes the soil to heat faster, resulting in faster insect development.

Carefully examine each site for signs of pest problems, such as circular yellow or brown spots, bare spots, or slow or unusual growth. If any one insect seems particularly abundant, count the number in a given area and collect a sample for identification. This may be the culprit. Look it up at the public library, or ask the staff at your local garden centre. If all else fails, send the bug for identification to one of the labs listed in the Sources section at the back of this book.

Choose one or two of your monitoring sites (particularly one with dying grass and no visible cause). Cut three sides of a one foot square in the sod at the edge of a damaged area, and take a peek underneath for grubs or other pests feeding on your roots. Count the numbers of each, and collect specimens for identification. One root feeder poses no immediate threat, but

The Coffee-Can Method is a great way to check for Chinch Bugs, and involve your family in environmentally sound monitoring practices.

some species are dangerous in low numbers.

Alternatively, mix a capful of liquid detergent in a pail of water and pour it over one of your monitoring sites with a sprinkling can. Sod webworms and other pests will appear on the surface where they can be detected and counted.

To detect chinch bugs, a common lawn pest, remove both ends from a large coffee can and push it into the sod. Fill the can with water. After about five minutes all of the bugs will float to the surface. The coffee-can treatment is a perfect opportunity to involve your kids in environmentally sound and enjoyable monitoring.

TROUBLESHOOTING:
When all else fails

If you have been following the maintenance programme outlined in this chapter, you shouldn't have a problem with weeds, disease, or insects. In fact, you may be astonished at the vigour of your lawn.

As a further preventive measure, you can also encourage pest-eating birds (see Chapter 4 for details) and introduce beneficial bugs such as ladybugs and praying mantis (see Suppliers).

However, if you discover clear signs of trouble - yellow or brown patches, mildew, etc. - when you are out on your monitoring saunter, see below for remedial action and least-toxic control methods.

INSECTS:

Ants
Ants are attracted to nutritionally poor, dry soils, low in organic matter. While they are natural aerators, they damage your lawn under their hills, and they damage

LEAST TOXIC REMEDIES:
All of the remedies listed have proven to be effective depending on the conditions and diligence of application. You can try any one, or group them for a multi-pronged attack. Some of the ingredients will already be available in your home, while others will require a trip to a gardening centre, or a call to one of the Suppliers listed in this book.

roots in the immediate vicinity of the ant-hill. The damage is not severe, however, and they are regarded more as a household nuisance.

You can apply sand, borax, bone meal, or diatomaceous earth to their mound openings. Commercial traps are available containing everything from borax and honey to peanut butter.

Generally, if you increase the organic matter in your soil by top-dressing with compost, your soil will retain more moisture and the ant problem will take care of itself.

Chinch Bugs

These tiny red nymphs turn grey and then develop wings as they mature. If you find more than 100 to 150 per square metre (10 to 15 per square foot) in any of your coffee can samplings, you are probably slacking off in your lawn maintenance duties.

Chinch bugs like lots of thatch, 2 cm (three-quarters inch) or more, accompanied by dry roots, and soil low in nitrogen (or too high in a chemical, highly soluble form of nitrogen, just to confuse things).

Aerate in spring and summer, and de-thatch in fall. Water deeply and infrequently in the mornings. Test and correct for nitrogen deficiencies.

However, if you find large, irregularly-shaped yellow patches of lawn turning to brown, and if hordes of chinch bugs show up in your coffee can float test, it's time to take more aggressive action.

Put a capful of dishwashing soap in a sprinkling can filled with water, and drench a problem area. Lay a piece of white flannel over the drenched area (an old bedsheet is perfect), and the bugs will cling to it as they

SOAP DRENCHES:

Household soap drenches can be made with liquid dishwashing detergents and water. They are used to flush bugs out of their habitats. Insecticidal soaps are high in fatty acids, making them toxic to insects. They are used to kill unwanted insects by direct applications to infested plants, or when mixed with water in a container, as final resting baths for hand-picked specimens. Soaps do not harm plants.

CAUTION: don't leave open containers of soap mixtures within the reach of children or pets.

try to get away from the soap. Fifteen to 20 minutes later, vacuum the flannel or rinse it off into a bucket filled with insecticidal soap (see Glossary). It may sound crazy, but it works, and kids will love to help.

Sod Webworm Moths

If you notice small whitish or dingy brown moths darting about, this is probably the adult sod webworm, which hatches from a caterpillar in heavy thatch. The caterpillars skeletonize and then cut off grass blades.

A healthy lawn is relatively safe from sod webworms if the larvae are present in small numbers, say, 20 or 30 in a square metre (2 or 3 per square foot). But if your lawn is compacted, thatchy and dry, even one of these insects can cause problems.

To check for sod webworms, use a soap drench of a capful of liquid detergent in a pail of water, and sprinkle a 60 cm square (2 foot square) area. The webworm caterpillars should crawl to the surface in five to ten minutes. Rake them up and drop them in a bucket of insecticidal soap.

Aerate, top-dress with endophytic grass seed, and de-thatch in fall. Re-seeding will repel webworms and fill in the damaged bare spots, crowding out weeds.

Most caterpillars like lawns that are hot and dry during the day. Irrigate and top-dress with 6 millimetres (a quarter inch) of screened, weed-free compost to help correct the problem.

These measures should take care of the problem, but as a last resort you can introduce beneficial nematodes (see Glossary) as a "natural" control (see Suppliers).

White Grubs

The larvae of the European Chafer, the June Beetle, and the Japanese Beetle show up when you monitor by lifting sod. The grubs are soft and white, with C-shaped bodies. They range in size from 6 to 75 millimetres (one-quarter to three inches) long. They are root feeders. If they are present in quantities larger than 50 to 100 per square metre (5 to 10 per square foot) they can cause patches of your lawn to turn brown and die.

The best defence against all three is a dense healthy lawn. De- thatch, aerate, and keep surface moisture to a minimum by watering deeply and infrequently. Japanese beetles particularly like moist soil for egg-laying. But their eggs often fail to hatch if surface soils are allowed to dry between irrigations. Dig out the entire root when weeding since grubs prefer weed roots to grass roots.

Milky Spore Disease, a naturally occurring bacterium, will control white grubs for years once well established in your soil. Milky Spore Disease is widely used in the United States, but is not yet registered for use in Canada. Lobby your local garden centre to start stocking it, and help get the registration ball rolling.

SLEUTHING FOR GRUBS: You'll be able to determine if white grubs are the cause of any dead patches of lawn by cutting three sides of a 1 ft. square in your lawn at the edge of the damaged area. Gently lift the cut corner, and peek at the roots.

For now, infestations causing large-scale damage can only be remedied by cutting your sod into squares and turning the pieces over. Thoroughly dig and add compost to the soil underneath. If you leave the grass roots exposed for an hour or two while adding the compost, birds will eat the grubs right off the sod. When digging is complete, replace the sod.

DISEASES:

All lawn diseases can be directly attributed to a deficiency in your lawn's ecosystem, so the best prevention is proper lawn care. Monitor weekly to diagnose and treat a problem at its early stages. Most diseases afflict lawns containing a large proportion of fine turfgrasses. Aerate and top-dress with one of the recommended disease-resistant ryegrasses.

Brown Patch

Brown patch is a fungus that likes heavy thatch, humid shaded areas, and high nitrogen levels. It appears as circular or crescent-shaped brown patches. De-thatch, aerate, cut down on nitrogen, and prune back shade trees and shrubs. Fill in dead patches with endophytic ryegrass seed.

Dollar Spot

This common lawn fungus thrives on lawns with too little nitrogen and too much moisture above the soil - both products of improper watering and thatch build-up.

Dollar spot appears as small, circular bleached dead spots of grass in spring or fall.

Aerate, de-thatch in fall, test for nitrogen levels, and amend accordingly with a slow-releasing organic product. Water in the mornings, and level out uneven spots in your lawn with topsoil to prevent puddles. Dollar spot also loves grass cut too frequently and too short (see Mowing on page 36). The problem will subside once corrective measures are taken.

Fusarium Blight (Frog-Eye)

This common fungus likes a combination of humid weather and excess nitrogen. It appears as a patch of brown dying grass with tufts of green grass in the middle. Reduce nitrogen applications and overseed

LAWN DISEASES:

Many lawn diseases can be attributed to overly moist, shaded areas that have been mowed too frequently and too short. Increase drainage by aerating and top-dressing with screened compost. Cut back shade trees, and water the grass in the early mornings, less often.

with endophytic ryegrass.

Mildew

Powdery mildew appears as a grey cobwebby or white powdery growth, mainly on the upper surface of the grass blade. This fungus is most severe in shaded, wet areas with poor circulation.

Aerate, prune back shade trees, and avoid watering in the evenings. Allow the soil to dry out between waterings. Fertilize and mow high with sharp blades.

Mushrooms

Mushrooms, commonly called toadstools, often appear in lawns during rainy spells in the summer. They are the above-ground growth of a fungus that is growing on underground organic matter - a buried stump or tree root. They are often a result of poor drainage or excessive shade.

They are harmless, and they can be removed by raking. No other method of control will kill them without damaging your lawn. Mushrooms tend to like slightly acidic and calcium-deficient soils. Test your pH balance and calcium content. Add dolomitic limestone and wood ashes to bring the pH up to 6.5.

WEEDS:

We hate to be accused of nagging, but most weed problems can be attributed to soil compaction, excessive thatch, improper mowing practices, and unbalanced pH and nutrient levels in your soil. If you keep your lawn healthy by practising the maintenance programme outlined in this chapter, you'll have very few problems with weeds.

However, if weeds exceed your tolerance levels, there are easy, chemical-free ways to control them.

Chickweed

This annual plant sends out tangled stems that root rapidly in slightly acidic soil under cool moist conditions.

Check pH and adjust for acidity, and hand-pull to their roots as soon as chickweed appears.

Clover

All clovers are extremely beneficial to lawns. They fix nitrogen in the soil, and are often planted as a green manure - a winter crop that is turned under in spring to fertilize the soil. Clovers attract beneficial nectar-feeding insects, and add texture and colour to your lawn. Clover is often added to lawn seed mixes purposely. Think twice before you decide to do away with this "weed."

Clover is an indication of alkaline soil, and can be controlled by increasing acidity.

If you are determined to rid your lawn of clover, make a solution of one part vinegar and one part liquid fertilizer (fish fertilizer is best) and squirt the patch with a spray bottle. The grass will initially turn brown with the clover, but the fertilizer will bring it back.

Crabgrass and Annual Bluegrass

If this pesky genus of lawn weed appears, it's a sign of nutrient-deficient soil, excessively frequent and close mowing, and poor aeration. Improve lawn maintenance. Test your soil, aerate,and top-dress with endophytic ryegrass,organic amendments, and lime as needed.

Creeping Charlie (Moneywort)

This "weed" is a member of the primrose family that spreads by trailing stems. Small coloured flowers bloom profusely in mid-summer above dark green leaves. The Aurea variety has golden leaves and makes

CLOVER:
PRO OR CON?

Clovers are actually extremely useful for lawns. They attract beneficial nectar-feeding insects, and fix nitrogen in your soil. In fact, clover is often added to seed mixes intentionally.
Pest or Guest?

a stunning ground cover.

Creeping Charlie likes moist shady areas. If you really want to rid your lawn of these beautiful visitors, increase drainage by aerating, de-thatching, and adding screened compost. Allow soil to dry in affected area between waterings.

Dandelions

Dandelions are considered to be beneficial herbs, high in vitamins A and C, iron and potassium. Dandelions also attract a natural microscopic predator, the parasitic wasp, that helps to keep down caterpillar, fly maggot, and earwig populations.

However, if you aren't impressed with these properties, you can control dandelions by increasing soil pH and digging them out to the root with a knife or narrow spade. Fill in cut areas with endophytic ryegrass seed to keep weed competition down. Cut the grass before your dandelions go to seed.

If dandelions appear along patio or sidewalk borders, consider planting fast-growing flowers to crowd them out. Check with your garden supply centre.

Plantain

Plantain can be used to make an anti-inflammatory poultice. If you have an aching joint, steam the leaves, wrap them in cotton cloth, and drape this over the affected area. It works wonders.

Plantain appears in slightly alkaline soil with poor drainage. Test pH and correct. Dig out the weeds to their roots (they are fairly shallow), aerate, and overseed with ryegrass.

Thistle

This prickly weed is difficult to eradicate. While some people are partial to its purple flower heads, many others dislike

THE DANDELION PATROL:

A few of the more zealous home owners we talked to spoke of picking off dandelion heads that had gone to seed - by hand! Their advice was to use a plastic bag to cover the head of the offender, and pinch it off while it is still in the bag. If you miss mowing the lawn before the weeds form seed heads, this may be worth a try.

CAUTION: avoid inhaling the seeds.

the thorns on the leaves.

Thistle has a deep root that cannot be destroyed easily: it must be dug out completely. Any little pieces left in the ground will produce new plants. Fill in the hole with topsoil and sprinkle with ryegrass seed.

It is not necessary - or environmentally desirable - to continue drenching your lawn in toxic chemicals. You and your family can enjoy a healthy beautiful yard that is organiclly maintained by following the five steps outlined above. And if a buttercup or primrose appears, don't panic. Make it the centrepiece for your next picnic.

CHAPTER 4:

CHEMICAL-FREE HOME GARDENS

If you want to be sure that you are not eating pesticides along with your vegetables, buy certified organic produce. Even better, grow your own. A few of your vegetables may go to bugs, but the sacrifice will be worth it. Plant a few extra, and almost all of your crop will survive unmolested to feed you, your family and friends deliciously and safely.

YOUR GARDEN PLOT:
A Place in The Sun

Vegetable gardens need plenty of sunlight, good soil, and good drainage. Pick a spot with a southern exposure, away from shady trees and buildings.

Prepare the soil as outlined in Chapter 2. But take note: plants differ in their pH and nutrient requirements. Before you add organic fertilizers or lime, investigate the specific requirements of the plants you intend to grow. Tomatoes need acid soil, for example, while cabbage needs alkaline soil.

As you dig your garden plot, leave the topsoil in raised beds for more effective feeding, weeding, and watering. Plant taller crops in the north rows, shorter ones in the south.

As you dig your plot and add manure and compost, we recommend that you leave the topsoil in raised beds or mounds. Raised beds make plants easier to feed, weed, and water. They ensure proper drainage. They also keep roots cooler in hot weather, and warmer in cool climes. If you make your beds small enough to reach the middle comfortably from each side, you eliminate soil compaction due to human traffic between rows. This minimizes aeration problems.

The raised beds or rows should run east west, with tall crops planted in the northern beds, shorter crops in the south.

COMPANION PLANTING:
With friends like these, you'll have fewer enemies

Companion planting is a basic principle of organic gardening. Many plants repel bugs, and provide natural protection if they are planted beside susceptible plants. Some plants help to feed their neighbours by making trace elements easily available to their roots.

For example, the roots of French Marigolds repel nematodes that infest many garden plants, including tomatoes and potatoes. Plant them throughout the garden, and in consolidated blocks in beds that will grow tomatoes next year.

Interplanting potatoes and collards reduces flea beetle damage. Garlic repels the larvae of many harmful insects, and can be planted next to anything except onions. Onions repel many species, and can be scattered throughout the garden.

On the other hand, some plants are actually bad for each other when planted too close together. Related plants like cauliflower and brocolli should also be separated to discourage bugs that like the whole family.

For in-depth information on the art of companion planting, see Louise Riotte's "Carrots Love Tomatoes" and Rodale's "Encyclopedia of Organic Gardening" listed in the Further Reading section in the back of this book.

PLANTING YOUR GARDEN:
As you sow, so shall you . . .

Make a map of your garden rows, marking the sections where your vegetables and companion flowers will be planted, north to south. Be sure to keep the map in a safe place for reference until next year's garden is planted. Now you are ready to sow.

Choose disease-resistant plant varieties, and varieties which are suited to your climate. Check with your local garden centre.

If you are growing from seed, buy seeds that have not been treated with fungicides or other chemicals. If you order from a catalogue, request chemical-free seeds.

Plant as recommended on the seed packet, indoors in sterile potting soil, or outdoors once the soil has warmed. If you are starting seeds indoors, be sure to "harden off" the seedlings. Start by putting the pots outside during the day and bringing them in at night for a few days. Then leave them outdoors overnight for a few days before actually planting them in your prepared beds.

Follow your gardening plan, planting companions next to each other, and separating related species to discourage bugs that are attracted to that family. Plant flowers throughout the vegetable garden to attract beneficial insects and birds that will feed on undesired garden raiders.

SEEDS AND PLANTS, THE PROPER CHOICE:

Plant selection is essential for healthy, sturdy crops. Be sure to choose disease and pest-resistant varieties that have been bred for your climate. This information will be right on the packet, or available from your seed dealer.

BUG–EATING BIRDS:
Winging-it

Erect supports for beans, tomatoes, peas, etc.,before you plant, so that the roots of your plant will not be damaged later.

If you are sowing seeds directly in the beds, place them close together, thinning them out as the plants require more space. Water gently with a sprinkling can, and mulch (see Mulching, next page). Keep mulches moist until seeds germinate, and you see the tiny plants push through.

Transplant seedlings as close to one another as possible to shade out weeds, and thin the seedlings as they require more room. Always transplant early in the day before the sun gets too hot to protect the roots while they are exposed. Plant quickly, and water the bed around each plant gently and thoroughly. Mulch around the seedlings.

Certain flowers attract birds that feed mainly on weeds and insects, not fruit, berries, or flower leaves. These birds belong to the **Fringillidae family,** which includes cardinals, purple and house finches, buntings, crossbills, grosbeaks, goldfinches, towhees, juncos, and the dozens of varieties of native sparrows.

Sunflower, marigold, cosmos, amaranthus, and portulaca all attract the right sort of winged pest control. Birds are attracted to the seeds of these flowers, but during the spring and summer they'll move on to consume great quantities of insects and weeds. The flowers must be allowed to go to seed, so don't whisk away blooms as they begin to droop. The plants listed not only attract birds, they also go to seed gracefully, so to speak.

PEST CONTROL
ON THE WING:
Birds that feed on garden pests are welcome visitors to any home. To attract these bug-eating birds, plant the flowers that make their gourmet list: marigolds, sunflowers, cosmos, amaranthus, and portulaca.

THE SEVEN-STEP MAINTENANCE PROGRAMME: How does your garden grow?

STEP ONE: Mulching
The Protective Blanket

Mulches are coverings laid directly on garden beds to keep weeds down, retain moisture and warmth in the soil, and hasten germination of seeds. Unless you live in a very wet and cool climate, mulches are generally a fantastic aid to the organic gardener. They cut maintenance time down to a fraction.

Mulches can be made from organic matter such as straw, grass clippings, sea-weed, compost, or sawdust. But avoid hay or unsterilized manures, which harbour weed seeds, and any matter which may have been treated with pesticides.

Organic mulches can be applied in thin layers over planted seeds to hasten sprouting of plants, placed around transplanted seedlings to cover beds, and spread on your beds after the fall harvest.

Mulches can also be made from inorganic substances such as black plastic or landscaping fabric. Our advice is to avoid them as their manufacture and disintegration creates environmentally harmful products.

Organic mulches add nutrients slowly to the soil as they break down. The disadvantage is that they may attract slugs, earwigs, and some fungi and moulds in cool, wet climates. In areas of the country with short or cool growing seasons, mulches can insulate the soil, keeping it cool and rotting the plant roots. In these conditions, it is better to water uncovered beds as needed instead of mulching.

Mulches of sawdust and wood chips are

a good idea along garden paths to keep weeds down.

STEP TWO: Watering
Soak the soil, not the foliage

Most gardens need a thorough soaking at least once a week. The water should soak the soil to a depth of 2.5 cm (1 inch) below the roots. Use a screwdriver or chopstick as a test probe, at least one day after watering. The soil should remain moist at root level throughout the season.

Water the soil, not the foliage. Perforated hoses work best. Set the water pressure so you get a dribble rather than a high spray.

Water early in the morning to avoid burning the foliage and to allow soaking-in time before nightfall. This will discourage slugs and other water-seeking pests. If your plants show signs of leaf wilt, water the surrounding soil immediately and readjust your watering schedule to prevent the soil from drying out between applications.

STEP THREE: Feeding
It is what it eats

Add soil amendments after the soil has warmed in spring, while you are doing your preparatory digging (see Chapter 2). But don't stop then. Even if your soil is perfectly balanced for pH and nutrients at the beginning of the season, keep adding manure and compost as your garden grows. These amendments can be added over or under organic coverings.

Use sterilized, well-rotted manure as a side-dressing for members of the cabbage family and all leafy crops. The exceptions are members of the legume family such as

WATERING:

Make sure that you water the soil, not the foliage of your garden plants. If the leaves and fruit are wet, they will burn as the sun evaporates the moisture. Dampness on the foliage will also increase the chances of disease.

peas and beans. Apply a thin line of the manure evenly under the drip-line of each plant (see Glossary) as follows:

Cabbage family: two to three weeks after transplanting and every week thereafter.

Leafy crops: three to four weeks after thinning out the bed and every week thereafter.

STEP FOUR: Aeration
The breath of life

Your soil needs oxygen throughout the growing season. Gently aerate your beds twice a month, being careful not to damage roots. Use a spiked roller, available at most garden supply stores, a trowel, or a hoe, and gently cultivate the soil around your plants. Add compost and water. .

Avoid soil compaction by minimizing foot traffic through your garden. Raised beds are useful for this purpose (see Your Garden Plot, page 49).

STEP FIVE: Preparing for Next Year
Cleanliness is next to ...

Clean up your garden in fall to help get rid of pests that lay eggs in leftover garden debris. Don't leave dead plants in your soil over the winter. Dig them up, and remove them to your compost pile.

Dig the soil under, adding composted manure. Add seaweed as a winter mulch, if it is available, or else straw.

STEP SIX: Green Manure
Winter Food, Spring Fodder

After you remove plant debris from the

SIDE-DRESSINGS:

To feed your plants with compost and manure throughout the season, apply a thin line of the organic matter in a circle around each plant below the outer-most foliage (the drip-line). When rain drips off the plant, it will fall onto the compost or manure, and take their nutrients into the soil.

garden in the fall, add compost and manure, dig the soil under, and plant a fast-growing green manure crop such as clover or ryegrass. This fall crop will provide your soil with nitrogen throughout the winter, and with organic matter when turned under in spring. It will protect topsoil from the erosion of winter snow, winds and rain, and increase absorptive and biochemical processes in your soil. Your garden centre or seed supplier can assist you in your choice of a green manure crop.

Plant as soon as possible after the last harvest, and at least one or two weeks before the first killing frost.

If root-feeders (grubs of June and Japanese beetles) have been a problem, avoid green manures for a season or two until the larvae have been eradicated. Instead, dig and turn your soil as long and as soon as the weather permits each season.

Plant companions next to each other, and

separate related varieties such as cauliflower and broccoli to discourage bugs. Keep a map of this year's garden, and take care not to rotate family members to each other's beds next season.

STEP SEVEN: Crop Rotation
Musical Beds

Keep your garden map from one season to the next so you can keep track of where everything was planted and rotate your crops accordingly. This involves keeping related plants separated, in both the same and consecutive years. Crop rotation helps to keep down bugs that feed on a particular family of plants. It also gives your soil a needed rest from the nutritional demands of any one family.

For example, carrots are unrelated to lettuce, and can be planted next season in this year's lettuce beds. Broccoli and cauliflower are related, and should not be rotated to each other's beds. Broccoli and cauliflower should also be planted a few rows from each other in the same season.

For excellent charts on crop rotation see "The Harrowsmith Northern Gardener" and Rodale's "Encyclopedia of Organic Gardening" (see Further Reading).

TIPS ON TRANSITION:
Weaning the Garden

If you have been using chemical fertilizers and pesticides in your garden, your soil is deficient in organic matter and some important trace elements. The "good" bugs have been destroyed, together with the micro-organisms in your soil that help to repel disease and make nutrients available to plant roots.

A solution is at hand: feed your soil. Add compost and sterilized manure during your spring digging session. Dig it in, add more, and dig it in again for a good month before planting. If this means planting a little late, plant a little late. Continue adding organic matter as side-dressing around your plants throughout the season.

At the same time, follow all the advice outlined in this chapter, including the addition of organic fertilizers as required. These amendments will help your soil and plants through withdrawal from their chemical diet.

TRANSITION TIP:

You may experience some problems during the transitional period. But avoid the temptation to use chemical pesticides, herbicides or fertilizers on your garden, or you will destroy the progress you have made.

TROUBLESHOOTING:
When Pests Persist

Monitor your garden weekly. Inspect your plants for signs of disease, bugs, and weed infestations.

WEEDS:

If you follow the maintenance programme and preventive measures described in this chapter, weeds should not be a serious problem.

If weeds appear, they may be an indicator that your soil is unbalanced nutritionally. An excellent guide to weeds as indicators of soil conditions can be found in Rodale's "Encyclopedia of Organic Gardening" (see Further Reading).

Pull the weeds out by their roots and take corrective measures to balance your soil. The easiest time for weeding is right after watering - the roots come away readily. Remove weed debris from the garden to prevent re-rooting.

INSECTS:

If you follow the maintenance programme and preventive measures described in this chapter, insects should not be a serious problem.

Reemay, a finely woven fabric made from polypropylene, is gaining popularity as a shield to insulate and keep bugs off garden beds. Again, its manufacture and decomposition poses environmental problems, so we do not recommend its use.

Some insects, most notably ladybugs and praying mantises, consume hundreds of harmful bugs. If they are not already residents of your garden, you can buy them and introduce them. They will stay around for as many years as they find prey to eat (see Suppliers).

For added protection, you can put collars around seedlings to prevent cutworm damage. These can be made of tin cans, tarpaper, or cardboard milk cartons cut to size. Bushy plants like lettuce won't tolerate collars, but most others benefit.

If you find a bug you don't recognize during monitoring, look it up in a good reference book, take a sample to your local gardening centre, or send a sample to a pest identification source listed in the Sources section at the back of this book.

Refrain from using pesticides: they destroy all insect life, including beneficial insects. Make or purchase mechanical traps and barriers. If all else fails use the organic pest controls outlined below.

Aphids (also see page 79)

Aphids are attracted to plants in soil that is poor in organic matter. Add compost and sterilized manure as side-dressings.

Encourage the presence of aphids' natural enemies: ladybugs, praying mantises, and warblers. Avoid pesticides, and add a bird bath or two. Plant nasturtiums, garlic, chives, coriander, and anise throughout the garden as repellents.

Hose off infested plants with pH-balanced soap (eg. Ivory, Shaklee) or an insecticidal soap. Apply dust of diatomaceous earth (see Glossary and Suppliers) with a small paint brush to leaves of the affected plant.

Make or purchase aphid traps (see Suppliers). Cover yellow pieces of cardboard with a sticky substance (paste-on Tree Tanglefoot or Stick'em) and hang them about the garden. Or place a yellow dish full of soapy water in the garden. Monitor your catch. If you're drowning too many beneficial bugs along with the aphids, remove the dishes.

An aphid predator is available that can be sprinkled over infected plants (see Suppliers). This beneficial nematode will not harm the host plant.

INSECTS THAT LOVE APHIDS:
There are many beneficial insects that feed on the "harmful" ones in your garden. Ladybugs and praying mantids will eat many times their own weight in aphids a day. If these "good" bugs have not yet set up housekeeping in your garden, buy and introduce them to their new home (see Suppliers).

Cabbage Worms and Cabbage Loopers

Cabbage worms and loopers like slightly acidic soil. They attack members of the cabbage family, peas, lettuce and tomatoes. Fight back by making your soil more alkaline. Apply wood ashes in a ring at the base of affected plants.

You can also plant mint, catnip, thyme, and rosemary as deterrents. Hose your plants with insecticidal soaps, or hand-pick the caterpillars. Scrape off egg clusters and put them in a dish of insecticidal soap. Use Bt, according to label instructions, as a last resort (see Glossary & Suppliers).

Corn Borers and Earworms

These borers and worms are attracted to corn, but also like beans, peppers, peas, potatoes, and tomatoes. Resistant plant varieties are available, such as Calumet sweet corn. As further prevention, apply a small dose of mineral oil (20 drops) to the inside of the tip of each ear of corn with a paint brush or eye-dropper, after the silks have wilted. If that doesn't work, pick them off by hand. Use Bt as a last resort.

Corn is a heavy feeder, using up a great amount of nitrogen. Interplant with legumes to keep the nutrient level balanced and the borers and earworms at bay. Rotate the crop in next year's garden.

Cutworms

These soil-dwelling curled worms love tender young transplants, especially from the cabbage family, but they won't pass up beans and tomatoes. For prevention, keep your garden free of weeds and grass during fall months when cutworms are laying their eggs.

Plant sunflowers. They're beautiful, and

they attract and trap cutworms. Tansy and marigolds repel cutworms. Place tarpaper, cardboard, or tin can collars around transplants, sunk into the soil to a depth of 2.5 cm (1 inch) to prevent the worms from reaching plant stems. Encircle plants with wood ashes or diatomaceous earth (see Suppliers).

Earwigs

These insects eat the larvae of many harmful insects, and only occasionally attack vegetables. However, if they become a problem, lay a hollow tube or a piece of bamboo with a few drops of water inside at one end of your garden. The earwigs will crawl inside during the night, and can be tapped into a bucket of soapy water in the morning.

Flea Beetles

Flea beetles are partial to corn, eggplant, potatoes, spinach, and tomatoes. They like hot, dry conditions. Keep your beds well irrigated in drought conditions. Interplant preferred varieties with garlic and other strong-smelling plants and flowers. Plant your crops thickly: beetles don't like shade.

Flea beetles can be controlled by handpicking, insecticidal soaps, a home-made spray of garlic and water, or a thin dusting of diatomaceous earth on the leaves. Keep weeds down, and rotate your crops next season.

June Beetle Larvae (a.k.a. white grubs)

These pre-historic looking soil grubs are most often found in soil that has recently been cleared for a garden. Their life-cycle as grubs can last three years, and they love roots of grasses and corn.

THE GARLIC SPRAY:

A home made repellant for flea beetles and many other insects, can be made with garlic and water. Place 10 cloves of peeled and chopped garlic in your blender with a litre of water and zap for thirty seconds. Fill a spary bottle with the solution, and spritz on affected plants.

If you find them during your spring digging - dig, dig, dig. The more the soil is exposed to the air, the faster the grubs will seek roots elsewhere - if the robins don't get them first.

These grubs are partial to chunks of potatoes, so bury a few in problem areas as bait, and dig them up a few days later. Plant geraniums with your corn as a natural repellant, and rotate corn with legumes next season.

If you find them when you are cleaning up the garden in the fall - dig, dig, dig, again. Turn your soil at least once a month until it is too cold to work. Add compost, and refrain from using a green manure during the winter, as the roots will keep the grubs feeding quite happily until next season.

Slugs and Snails

These slimy gastropods will eat almost anything in your garden, but they are easy to control. Place a saucer of beer in the soil so that the rim is at ground level. The suds-loving creatures will crawl right in. Place a depressed dish of brewer's yeast in the garden. The slugs will pig out, bloat and die.

You can also spread diatomaceous earth in a circle around plants.

Make collars of window screen to keep the slugs from climbing stems. Leave a board or cabbage leaf at garden corners overnight as a trap. The slugs crawl under the shelters, and you can remove and destroy them in the morning.

Don't use slug baits sold in stores. Slugs will eventually detoxify it and breed resistant sluglets. As well, your pets are at risk if they eat the bait.

SLUG TIPS:

Slugs love suds! They will make every effort to crawl into a shallow dish of beer if it is buried to the rim in your garden. You can hand pick the inebriated beasties out of the brew, and dispose of them.

Squash Bugs

These bugs love cucumbers, squash, and pumpkins. Companion plant these vegetables with nasturtiums, radishes, and marigolds. Place boards or shingles near the infested plants to trap the bugs overnight.

Squash bugs lay their eggs on the underside of the leaves in early summer. Look for egg clusters, scrape them off, and squash them or place them in a container of soapy water. Rotate your crops.

Thrips

These tiny dark thread-like insects like flowers, beans, and most weeds. Keep weed levels down, and remove crop thinnings and weed debris from the garden as soon as they are harvested.

A mulch of aluminium foil repels thrips. Place a flat circle around the plant with a slit cut for the stem. Apply dormant oil to the leaves of preferred plants (see Glossary and Suppliers). Beneficial nematodes that destroy thrips are also available.

Tomato Hornworms

These lime green worms prefer tomatoes, dill, eggplant, peppers, and potatoes. They reach 1 cm (1/2 inches) in length and are easily controlled by hand-picking. Plant marigolds, borage and nicandra as natural deterrents.

Brachanoid wasps attach themselves in white oval cocoons to the ends of the hornworms. If you see these cocoons on a worm, don't destroy them. The hatching wasps will do more than their share of pest control.

DISEASES:

Diseases in vegetable gardens are relatively rare. They most often attack tomatoes and members of the cabbage family such as broccoli and cauliflower.

The best fed and best tended plants tend to suffer least, so keep your soil and plants healthy.

Most diseases appear in mid to late season, when the weather is hot, foliage is dense, and disease-spreading insects (most notably the aphid) are moving from plant to plant. Be careful not to touch uninfected plants after handling diseased ones. Remove organic mulches a short distance from plant stems until the weather gets drier.

Bacterial Diseases

Bacterial diseases appear in hot humid weather, and attack non-resistant varieties. Choose resistant plants.

If diseases appear, destroy all affected plants, rotate your crops, and buy fresh seed next year.

Blight causes pea stems to turn purple or black at ground level. Small water-soaked spots appear on leaves and pods.

Bacterial ring affects potatoes, turning leaf edges inward. A dark ring appears on the tubers just inside the skin.

Soft rot affects lettuce, cabbage, and carrots, turning them soft and pulpy.

Fungal Diseases

Fungal diseases include clubroot (cabbage family), black leg (cabbage and tomatoes), and downy mildew (onions, lettuce, and peas). Like bacterial diseases, they appear in hot, humid weather.

DON'T SPREAD DISEASE:

Be careful to wash your hands thoroughly after handling diseased plants, especially before you tend to their uninfected neighbours. Dip any garden tools that have come in contact with diseased foliage in denatured alcohol.

Again, choose resistant varieties. Thin out seedlings and mature plants to promote good air circulation, remove mulches, and destroy all affected plants. Aerate beds, and rotate crops for next year's garden.

There is nothing so delicious as vegetables eaten moments after they are picked from your garden. And there is nothing so reassuring as knowing that you have raised them organically. Many gardeners in North America have practised organic gardening for decades and have found that while a few plants are sacrificed to pests, more than enough vegetables reach their tables, harvested from rich, healthy and safe soil.

CHAPTER 5:

ORGANIC LANDSCAPING

Ornamental shrubs and trees can grace your grounds in good health without the use of chemicals. As with lawns and gardens, the key to healthy, pest-resistant plants is healthy soil. Review Chapter 2 before following the advice in this chapter.

Choose varieties suited to your climate, soil, and light conditions. Your local nursery will help. Ask for varieties which have been bred for resistance to disease.

Choose individual plants carefully as well. Before you buy, examine them for signs of disease and pest damage. Don't accept a specimen with broken branches, scraped bark, or a ruptured root ball. You'll be asking for maintenance chores in the near future.

For advice on roses, check the special section in this chapter.

PLANTING:

Select a spot with

adequate sun and good drainage. Create a shallow well around the trunk at planting time, and wrap young trees with burlap for protection.

SOIL PREFERENCE:
Coffee, Tea, or Bone Meal?

Most evergreens (cedars, rhododendrons, azaleas, yews, junipers) like slightly acidic soil that is not too high in nitrogen.

Deciduous trees and shrubs (those that lose their leaves in winter) like soils that are richer in nitrogen (organic, of course) and organic matter supplied by compost. Proper drainage is essential. Some prefer slightly acidic soils (e.g. apple, cherry, oaks), while others do best in alkaline conditions (e.g. crabapple). Check with your nursery.

A soil test is necessary to determine the pH and nutritional balance of your soil before you add lime or specific nutrient amendments. Check the listing of soil-testing labs in the back.

PLANTING:
Right Time, Right Place

Plant shrubs and trees in early spring before new growth appears, or in fall, during their dormant period. Spring planting gives plants with delicate root systems a chance to establish themselves during the warm summer months. Be sure to select the spot carefully, in adequate sun and in an area with good drainage.

The importance of protecting the roots before planting can't be over-emphasised. Purchase all trees and shrubs when you are ready to plant to avoid exposing roots to the air. If this is not possible, coat the roots with mud and stand them in the shade. Mudding also protects the roots if you are planting on a hot, windy day. Alternatively, dig a temporary trench and bury the roots.

To plant, dig a hole deep and wide enough so the roots will not be cramped. But don't get carried away! The hole needs to be only slightly deeper and wider than the plant's root spread.

Recent research has proven that for most varieties of shrubs and trees, it is not a good idea to add fertilizers, peat moss or other soil boosters to the soil filling your hole. Roses and fruit trees are the exception.

With the plant in place, fill half the hole with topsoil and water. When the water has seeped in, add the remaining earth and tamp it down firmly. Apply a mulch around the trunk, but not touching it (see Mulching, page 53). Water again. Create a shallow well with earth around the trunk after planting to assist with irrigation (see Watering, page 73).

Trees should be staked only if they are planted in windy spots.

Young trees with thin bark (maples, beeches, birches, etc.) benefit if their trunks are wrapped in burlap for protection against sunscald, windburn, and certain types of tree borers. Use 15 cm (6 inch) strips of burlap with brown waxed freezer paper on the inside. Starting at the bottom, wrap up the trunk into the branches (see Illustration, page 67) The wrapping may be left on for one year. After that, bark will begin to decay.

THE THREE–STEP MAINTENANCE REGIME: for Beautiful Organic Landscaping

STEP ONE: Pruning
Cut for growth

Trees and shrubs need pruning for various reasons:

- to thin overly-dense growth,
- to correct or repair damage,

- to encourage fruit and flower production,
- to direct or control growth,
- to help a transplanted tree or shrub adjust to its new surroundings.

The season for pruning varies with the type of plant and the results you wish to achieve (see Shrubs, Hedges, and Fruit Trees, below).

Many home-owners pull out the chemical arsenal if their trees and shrubs are doing poorly when a good hair-cut will solve the problem. Removing dead or diseased branches is the best remedy.

A few general pointers on pruning shrubs, hedges and fruit trees follow (for more details see Further Reading section).

Tools

Always use the proper tool for the job, and make sure the cuts are clean, not jagged. For branches thinner than 1 cm (1/2 inch) in diameter, use hand pruning shears. For hardwood branches larger than 4 cm (1 1/2 inches) use a pruning saw. For branches of intermediate size, use lopping shears. If you are pruning a diseased plant, dip the cutting tool in denatured alcohol after use.

Shrubs

Shrubs that bloom from buds formed the previous season (azalea, dogwood, lilac, wisteria, climbing roses, and rhododendron) should be pruned immediately after flowering. Remove weak and dead branches, and cut back older ones lightly to make a well-shaped plant.

Remove the flowers of rhododendrons as they pass their prime, just behind the flower head. This will save plant energy and ensure new blossoms for next season.

Shrubs that form their buds from the current season's growth (clematis, cranberry, bush roses, honeysuckle) should be pruned during the dormant period in winter or early spring.

Neglected shrubs are often full of suckers, riddled with weak growth, or misshapen. They may need to be cut back almost to the ground. This extreme surgery is practised in early spring. Be strong of heart: new tops will sprout from the cut branches during the season, and can be thinned to produce a shapely plant.

Hedges

Keep hedges trimmed whenever new growth reaches 5 to 7.5 cm (2 to 3 inches) throughout the season. Keep shears sharp. Use a string stretched between stakes of equal height as a guide to keep the top of the hedge even, and hold the shears flat against the hedge while working.

Cut hedges in a bevel shape rather than trimming them straight up and down on the sides. Trim to make the hedge one and a half times wider at the bottom than the top.

Trim out dead wood and diseased branches as they appear. Burn the diseased cuttings. Check local ordinances, and use a barbecue in a pinch.

Fruit Trees

Young trees can be pruned in midsummer, but more mature trees should be cut back in March or April. During the fruit-bearing years you only need to remove weak or diseased wood, thin the branches,

HEDGE SHAPE:

Cut hedges so that they are curved rather than straight up and down on the sides. The top of the curve should be 1 1/2 times smaller than the thickness at the bottom.

and control the height and width of the tree. Do this every year to encourage good-sized, high-colour fruit.

STEP TWO: Fertilizing
Food for Bloom

Fertilize fruit trees in the early spring or fall after the foliage has dropped. Use a natural nitrogen source (fish fertilizer is best). Start with a low dose of 5 ml diluted in 23 litres (1 tsp in 5 gallons) of water at planting, and increase the concentration by 5 ml (1 tsp) each year, to a maximum of about 1 litre (1 quart) for full size trees, and 0.5 litre (half a quart) for dwarf varieties. Keep a record of your annual dose. Apply fertilizers to well outside the drip line, to ensure nourishment for roots.

Mulch with compost around the base of the trees for moisture retention and continued feeding.

Evergreen transplants enjoy an occasional top-dressing of well- rotted manure or compost in late fall or early winter. Mulch with evergreen boughs, oak leaves, peat moss, and grass cuttings. Use nitrogen-rich fertilizer to promote acidity. Check at the nursery for specific fertilizer needs. You can also have your soil tested for specific nutrient deficiencies as outlined in Chapter 2.

Lilacs are heavy feeders and need fertilizing every year. Apply a side-dressing of compost to the drip line in spring. Lilacs like acidic soil, so apply a mulch of hay, leaves, pine needles, or grass clippings, but avoid clippings from pesticide-treated lawns.

NOTE: Keep a record of the annual dose of fertilizer given to each tree.

STEP THREE: Watering
A drink in time ...

All trees should be watered immediately after transplanting. Water the soil, never the foliage.

Proper drainage is essential. Create a slight mound around the trunk when you plant, or leave a slight depression in the soil in a 60 cm (2 foot) circle around the trunk to create a well.

Mulches can be applied to retain moisture, but should not touch the trunks (see page 53 for details about Mulching).

Most species don't need watering beyond the first weeks. But in periods of drought, all newly transplanted trees and shrubs should be watered throughout their first two seasons. Soak the soil (not the foliage) thoroughly.

ROSES:
By any other name ...

Roses seem to be the most popular plant used in landscaping Canadian homes, and thus deserve a special section in this book. As with all species you plant, choose disease-resistant varieties suited to your soil and climate. If your climate is damp or severe in winter, choose a hardy species.

Teas and Hybrid Tea Roses like the Peace and Arlene Francis are favoured for their large single blooms, but they are the least hardy of the roses and therefore the most difficult to keep healthy in Canadian climates.

Floribunda Roses are disease-resistant and stand up to cold much better. They produce clusters of flowers, and bloom throughout the season.

Grandiflora varieties like the Queen Elizabeth have longer and thicker stems,

ROSE HARDINESS IN DESCENDING ORDER:

- **Shrub roses;**
- **Grandiflora roses;**
- **Multiflora roses;**
- **Hybrid Teas;**
- **Teas.**

If you expect your rose bushes to survive cold winters and hot humid summers, try some of the 'hardies'.

When planting roses, dig a hole in your prepared trench slightly larger than the diameter of the spread roots, and just deep enough to bury the bud graft. Gently spread the roots in a skirt over a cone of soil in the bottom of the hole, and fill in gently with topsoil.

NOTE:
Some growers insist that the graft be 2" below the surface to prevent frostbite, while others insist it be 2" above the soil to prevent suckers. Either way, in climates that have winter temperatures

making them hardier still. Your nursery or catalogue will provide you with the choices available in your area.

Shrub roses are the hardiest and often the most fragrant. They over-winter well in Canadian climates, and may be planted in borders with deciduous shrubbery like forsythia. They bear attractive but modest-sized blossoms. Rugosa rose is a family of vigorous shrubs that produce large fragrant blossoms almost continually through the season.

Rugosa roses also attract birds that eat garden bugs. They are resistant to insects and diseases and require no pruning or pampering. They are considered the 'work horse' of the rose world. Hansa, Rubra, and Explorer are popular varieties.

PLANTING ROSES:

Roses, being roses, require special treatment. They need sun, good air circulation, and slightly acidic soil with a pH between 6 and 5. Full sun for eight hours a day is best, but six hours of morning sun should be sufficient.

Your preparatory trench should be 60 cm (2 feet) deep for superior results in the long-term. Dig a few centimetres (inches) of the trench and save the topsoil. Dig the rest, and discard the soil, sprinkling it on your compost pile. Mix the reserved topsoil with topsoil and 125 ml (one-half cup) of our special rose food (see below) and return it to the bed, filling the trench to the surface. Allow the prepared soil to settle for two weeks before planting in that spot.

Examine the roots of the rose bush and prune away any damaged sections. Long straggly roots should also be cut back, and the tips of most others removed.

Dig your hole for planting slightly larger than the diameter of the spread roots and barely deep enough to bury the bud graft. Save all of the prepared soil when digging this hole. Create a cone-shaped mound at the centre of the hole at the desired depth for planting.

Place the bush on the mound, gently spreading the roots in a skirt over it. Continue adding the topsoil mix. When the hole is half filled, add a pail full of water. When the water has seeped away, fill the hole with your soil mix to ground level and tamp down firmly. Water again, gently.

Prune the canes 15 to 20 cm (6 to 8 inches) above the soil level. This may seem brutal, but your rose will live a longer, pest-free life as a result.

MAINTENANCE OF ROSES:

Roses need lots of water in dry seasons. Water the soil, not the foliage. Water deeply to the root depth - probe with a sharpened chop-stick to check this - in the mornings of sunny days from a slowly dribbling hose. Organic mulches are best in dry, hot areas, and fabric is recommended for wet areas.

Once planted, all roses will love our own special blend of (5 - 7 - 6) rose food made from 42 % blood meal, 36 % super phosphate or bone meal, 9.5 % sulphate of potash, 7.5 % kelp meal, and 5 % Sulpomag. You can make this up yourself or

below 10°F, roses must be protected with 8" of soil mounded at the base of the plant well before the first frost.

Rose FOOD:
OUR SECRET RECIPE!

This is our own secret blend for best-blooming healthy roses. With this publication, we decided to share it with the world! You can make it up yourself, or purchase it at Loblaws and subsidiaries:

- 42% blood meal;
- 36% super phosphate or bone meal;
- 9.5% sulphate of potash;
- 7.5% kelp meal;
- 5% Sulpomag.

purchase it pre-mixed (see Suppliers).

For Teas and Hybrid Teas gently scrape the soil at the base of the bush to the drip line with a fork. Sprinkle 125 ml (one-half cup) of the blend on the area and water gently. Repeat using 190 ml (three-quarters cup) just before or at blooming (late June-early July) and replace mulch if used. Apply 190 ml (three-quarters cup) again in very late fall, after all the leaves have dropped and just before you mound your plants for winter protection.

For climbers, bush roses, multiflora and grandifloras, double the above application rates.

Winter protection is essential. Where the temperature may fall below -11 degrees C. (10 degrees F.), mound soil around the plants to a depth of at least 20 cm (8 inches). Draw the canes upright with ties that will not bite into them, and trim them all to 75 cm (30 inches). Once the ground has frozen, you may apply mulches of straw, leaves, or garden refuse over the mounded soil. If you live in an area that is likely to experience cold winter winds, a burlap wrap or shield for the canes is advised.

Winter coverings, including mulches, should be removed a couple of weeks after the last frost has past, before spring growth starts. Let the soil surrounding the plants dry out in the spring sun until summer mulches are needed.

PREVENT ROSE DISEASE:

Buy resistant varieties, plant in well drained and sunny spots, plant in areas of good air circulation, and water the soil not the foliage

ROSE DISEASES:

Black Spot

Black spot, which looks like its name, is a fungus that attacks the leaves of roses. The spots are actually the spore cells of the disease.

All infected leaves should be removed and destroyed immediately, preferably by burning. Use your barbecue if necessary.

To prevent black spot, plant roses in full sun and increase air circulation around bushes by pruning if they are next to a building. Remove organic mulches from the stems and use landscape fabric instead. Water the soil, not the leaves. Water in the mornings, and probe with a chopstick to make sure watering is necessary.

In fall, rake fallen leaves, grass clippings and other plant debris. Debris serves as an overwintering home for disease.

Powdery Mildew

Like black spot, this fungus likes over-damp conditions. It is a powdery white growth that covers the tops of leaves as well as young shoots. Infected leaves become twisted and red.

Plant resistant varieties in full sun, and observe proper watering practices. Allow your soil to dry almost completely to root level before watering. Water the soil, not the foliage, in early mornings.

Thin out your plants and prune roses to ensure good air circulation. Promptly remove and destroy all infected parts.

For other rose pests, see Troubleshooting, below.

TROUBLESHOOTING:
Organic
out-manoeuvering
to prevent pests
and disease

There are many ways and means to deter pests before they do damage to your trees and shrubs. Burlap wrap, (see page 69) in the Planting section, is a good preventive measure against all crawlers. You can also apply whitewash made with lime and water or watered down latex paint to protect tree trunks against sunscald and cold in winter months. Whitewash also repels certain borers and worms.

Prevent worms and caterpillars from crawling to leaves by applying a protective sticky band to the trunk in fall and spring. Use Tree Tanglefoot, or another commercially available product made for this purpose (see Glossary). Leave no gaps or bridges for insects to cross.

For protection against infestations of aphids, red bug, scale, red spider mites, and thrips on most trees and bushes (roses too), spray the entire plant with dormant or miscible oil in early spring before any buds open (see Glossary). The sprays are available at most nursery and gardening supply stores, but some contain highly toxic additives such as sulphur, copper, and arsenic, and should be avoided. Spray in early morning to allow proper drying time. Note that oil cannot be used on all trees species. Read the label. Spray again in fall to kill eggs laid to over-winter.

Attract pest-eating birds by planting certain flowers (see Bug-Eating Birds, page 52). Purchase and introduce beneficial insects such as ladybugs, praying mantis, dragonflies from one of the suppliers listed in the back. They'll eat many times their weight in harmful bugs, and will stay in your garden as long as there is food for them (often for years). They are definitely worth the investment.

Good housekeeping is essential. Pick up all dropped blossoms and fruit as they fall. Remove and destroy all diseased growth as soon as it appears, but don't add it to your compost pile.

SMOTHERING PROTECTION:

Dormant or miscible oils can be sprayed onto roses, fruit trees, and other trees and shrubs to smother over-wintering scale, aphids, spider mites, and other pests. Some commercially available oils are mixed with sulphur, copper or arsenic. Read the label, and avoid those mixed with these toxic substances.

Monitor your shrubs and trees weekly for signs of bug infestations, leaf curl, blight, and other problems. Send any bugs that you are unsure of to the pest identification labs listed in the back (see Sources). Then, treat them organically with the troubleshooting methods listed below.

Commercially available traps for certain pests can be used to capture specimens for identification (see Suppliers).

INSECTS:

Aphids

These insects love just about any plant, and seem to flock to rose bushes.

High nitrogen levels in soil encourage several aphid species. Check your soil, and amend accordingly with slow-releasing organic fertilizers.

A healthy jet from a hose will temporarily remove aphids from leaves. But don't do this to roses because it will encourage disease. Rub rose leaves between your thumb and forefinger to kill the pests, or spray with insecticidal soap.

Aphids shy away from plants that are mulched with a layer of heavy aluminum foil. Place a large circular disc of foil flat on the ground around the trunk or stem.

Mix diatomaceous earth with water and brush it on both sides of infested leaves. The sharp edges of this powder pierce the bodies of the aphids, killing them. Select diatomaceous earth products that do not contain toxic additives such as rotenone.

You can also buy beneficial nematodes and aphid predators, but these need ample water to remain active. Other natural predators include lady beetles, praying mantises, parasitic wasps, house finches, warblers,

WOUND PREVENTION: When mowing, edging, or pruning around ornamentals, be careful not to wound your plants. Borers and other bugs will use any cuts in the bark as points of entry.

and bushtits. The insects in this list can be ordered from one of the suppliers listed in the back, and introduced to your landscaped area.

Borers

Borer larvae tunnel into wood, weakening and eventually killing the tree or shrub. Borers are indiscriminate: they like apple, ash, azalea, dogwood, flowering cherry, laurel, lilac, maple, oak, peach, plum, poplar, roses, and willow trees.

Make sure that the plant you purchase is uninfested, then take preventive measures. Wrap young trees with burlap and waxed freezer paper, and renew the wrap as necessary for at least two years after transplanting. Place an unbroken band of a sticky substance such a Tree Tanglefoot around the base of the tree to prevent the borers from crawling up the tree.

Borers gain entry through wounds, so be careful with your tools and lawnmowers. If you cause a wound, scrape it clean and treat with a tree dressing or pruning paint, available at your gardening centre.

Encourage the presence of woodpeckers, crows, vireos, and wasps, all of which destroy their share of borers. A mail-order beneficial nematode called Scan Mask will destroy borers if spread directly into their holes (see Suppliers).

Canker Worms and Loopers

These crawlers are recognizable by their characteristic form of locomotion: they extend forward then pull their hind body up in a loop.

Canker worms and loopers attack fruit and shade trees in spring and fall. Apply a sticky band such as Tree Tanglefoot, Tack-Trap, or Stick'em around the trunk to keep

NOCTURNAL RAIDING: Tent caterpillars are best disposed of after the sun has gone down and they have returned to their nest. This only works early in the season, however, as with age they have been known to stay out all night to play.

the females from climbing up to lay their eggs. Apply in February and October, and ensure that there are no gaps in the circle. Bt can also be used as a last resort.

Tent Caterpillars

The tent caterpillar spins a familiar tent-like nest in the branches of apple, flowering cherry, and other deciduous trees. Your best defence is to remove the tents with a pole and burn them. Remove the tents at night, when most are inside seeking shelter. The exposed caterpillars will fall prey to local predators.

Remove the tents as soon as they appear. Once the caterpillars reach a length of 2.5 cm (1 inch), they stay out to play at night, making them harder to control.

Prune twigs bearing brown, hard, foamy egg collars in winter or very early spring. Use Bt, if all else fails.

Gypsy Moths

The larvae of this moth are responsible for extensive damage to fruit, ornamental and shade trees in eastern Canada. The brown, hairy caterpillar grows to 5 cm (2 inches), and feeds nocturnally throughout June and July.

To control, wrap burlap around the trunk of your tree in several lengths, and fold over the top to form a shelter. Worms will be attracted to this sheltered area when it is time to pupate. Crush the caterpillars inside the band, or remove the burlap and shake the pests into a bucket of water topped with one quarter cup of kerosene.

Scrape off the tan egg clusters, which are laid in 2.5 cm (1 inch) ovals on branches.

You can also mail-order a natural predator called trichogramma wasp, which comes prepared on small sheets of sandpaper in its egg stages. Place the sheet of sandpaper in a branch of the affected tree and the predators do the rest.

Leafrollers

These caterpillars attack fruit trees and roses, causing the leaves to roll up as they feed. Spray the plant with dormant oil before the buds open, as outlined in the Prevention section. Remove affected branches if the damage is not too widespread, and destroy them. Bt can also be used.

Cedar Leaf Miner

The larvae of this insect feed on the tips of foliage of white cedars, causing them to turn brown. Adults are tiny grey moths which take flight when foliage is disturbed in June and July. Clip infested hedges and small bushes before June. Destroy the clippings, burning them where municipal ordinances permit. The barbecue may come in handy for this task. This reduces the population before the adults emerge. Leafminers seldom cause significant damage. Clipping is a sufficient control.

Scale Insects

Many different species of these minute insects attack branches and trunks of trees in Canada. Spray dormant oil in late April.

Spider Mites

These common pests appear as tiny red dots on the underside of foliage, on roses, evergreens, and most shrubs. Hose your plants to wash away mites and their webs.

For seriously infected plants, apply a solution of flour and buttermilk, mixed until it is sticky. This mix should be used after leaves have matured.

Beneficial nematodes are available by mail order. They can be placed directly in the branches of infested plants.

DISEASES:

Most bacterial and fungal diseases can be kept in check by planting your ornamentals in their preferred soil and location. Over-damp beds invite diseases and should be avoided.

Plant trees with adequate air flow around the branches, not too close to buildings or fences. Don't use chemical fertilizers or pesticides. They can destroy the "police" microorganisms that naturally control bacteria and fungi.

If signs of disease appear, immediately remove and destroy all affected growth. Remove organic mulches from around the base of the plant to allow air to get at the roots. If dampness and disease persist, call it a day, and plant new, resistant varieties. Use landscape fabric rather than organic mulches.

Beautiful landscaping helps to make a house feel like a home. If you do it organically, you won't have to worry about keeping pets or small family members off your grounds for fear of pesticide contact.

If you have hired a service to care for your lawn, trees and shrubs, talk to your contractor about the method outlined in this book and insist that your grounds be maintained without the use of toxic chemicals. Many companies are starting to offer "organic" service, so shop around if your current contractor seems less than enthusiastic.

If you take good care of your grass, trees and shrubs by providing healthy soil and instituting good maintenance practices, they will give you problem-free beauty in a chemical-free environment for years to come.

GLOSSARY:

ACIDIC:

Strictly speaking, a pH below 7. However, soil is normally slightly acidic, with a pH of about 6.5, and the term acidic is used to describe soils with a pH lower than this. Acidic soils are usually found in areas of high rainfall.

ALKALINE:

Again, strictly speaking, a pH above 7. But since soil is normally slightly acidic, soil with a pH of 7 or higher is described as alkaline.

BENEFICIAL NEMATODES:

Live organisms that transfer diseases to insects, including root weevils, aphids, root maggots, and spider mites. Available in mail-order packages designed for specific bugs. Need healthy amounts of water to keep active.

B.T. 'BACILLUS THURINGIENSIS':

Live bacteria that is highly selective, targeting only members of soft-bodied, leaf- eating caterpillars. Some commercial formulations contain pesticides.

DIATOMACEOUS EARTH.

A non-toxic flour-like powder made from fossilized skeletons of micro-organisms called diatoms. The sharp edges of the powder cuts the bodies of insects, causing them to lose their waxy coating and die. Do not inhale or ingest. Wear a paper mask, available at hardware stores, and gloves. Some commercially available products may contain chemical pesticides.

DORMANT OR MISCIBLE OILS:

Oils that mix with water when heated or agitated. They are used as a smothering agent for scale, worms, etc., that attack trees. Some commercially available formulations contain toxic substances such as sulphur, copper, or arsenic. Read the label.

DRIP LINE:

The line on the soil below the outermost foliage of a plant. Rain that is shed will first fall along this line.

ENDOPHYTIC FUNGI:

Symbiotic fungi found naturally in tissues of certain grasses which resist attacks from certain insects and diseases, including sod webworm, billbug larvae, chinch bugs, and aphids. They do not harm the host plant.

FUNGICIDE:

Any substance that kills fungi.

HERBICIDE:

Any substance that kills plants.

INSECTICIDAL SOAP:

A soap high in fatty acid content that kills insects. Not harmful to plants.

INSECTICIDE:

Any substance that kills insects.

INSECT TRAPS:

Store-bought or home-made devices for luring and trapping harmful insects. For example, a yellow sticky-surfaced card that traps aphids which come into contact.

MULCH:

A soil covering that inhibits the growth of weeds, retains moisture for the crop plant, and protects roots from severe temperature changes. Organic mulches may include grass clippings, spoiled hay, leaves, evergreen needles, straw, seaweed or sawdust. Inorganic mulches include clear or black plastic and landscaping fabric.

PESTICIDE:

An herbicide, fungicide, or insecticide which kills plants, diseases, and insects.

SOAP DRENCHES:

Soap and water solutions used to flush chinch bugs, cutworms, and other bugs to the soil surface. Also used as an organic pesticide applied directly to plants in a water solution. Can be made from a mild, pH-balanced soap such as Ivory or Basic H.

SIDE-DRESSING:

A method of mid-season fertilizing. Nutrients (fertilizers or compost) are spread on soil beside plants, usually under the drip line, for slow release of nutrients.

TOP-DRESSING:

A method of fertilizing established crops, especially lawns. Well shredded and screened compost or organic fertilizers are sprinkled directly onto plantation using a spreader to achieve even distribution.

TREE TANGLEFOOT:

A sticky compound painted in a band around tree trunks to prevent insects from climbing the trunk. Apply over a band of latex paint. Stick'em and Tack-Trap are other commercially available brands.

ORGANIC SUPPLIERS:

Many nurseries, garden centres, grocery stores and hardware stores are starting to stock a more complete line of products for organic gardeners. If your local outlet is behind in its efforts, some gentle persuasion will most likely get things going. In the meantime, here is a small sample of outlets that carry some or all of the products we have recommended.

Some of these suppliers fill mail orders throughout Canada. Some also carry traditional chemical fertilizers and pesticides, so be specific in your orders.

BRITISH COLUMBIA

Applied Bionomics Ltd.
11074 West Saanich Road
Sidney, B.C. V8L 3X9
(604) 656-2123
Carries insect parasites, predators, nematodes against thrips, aphids, and spider mites. Will mail across the country.

Avant Gardener
1448 Marine Drive
West Vancouver, B.C. V7J 1B7
(604) 926-8784
Organic suppliers

Foxglove Farms
C47 Crofton Road
R.R. 3
Ganges, B.C. V0S 1E0
(604) 537-5531
Carries all organic fertilizers, diatomaceous earth, Tanglefoot, dormant oils, manures.

ALBERTA

Golden Acres Garden Centre
620 Goddard Avenue N.E.
Calgary, Alberta T2K 5X3
(403) 274-4286
Carries bone meal, blood meal, super phosphate, traps, and manures. Also has outlets in Edmonton and Medicine Hat.

SASKATCHEWAN
Early's Farm and Garden Centre
2615 Lorne Avenue
Box 3024
Saskatoon, Saskatchewan S7K 3S9
(306) 931-1982. Call toll-free
February 1 to July 1 inside
Saskatchewan, **1-800-667-1159.**
*Carries diatomaceous earth,
Tanglefoot, dormant oils, pest-
resistant grass seed, organic
fertilizers, Bt, etc. Catalogue
free inside Canada.*

MANITOBA
Modern Organics
1373 Spruce Street
Winnipeg, Manitoba R3E 2V8
(204) 775-3433
Carries biological fertilizers.

T and T Seeds
111 Lombard Street
Box 1710
Winnipeg, Manitoba R3C 3P6
(204) 943-8483
*Carries pest-resistant seeds,
diatomaceous earth, Bt, and
organic fertilizers. Catalogue $1.*

ONTARIO
Better Yield Insects
Box 3451, Tecumseh Station
Windsor, Ontario N8N 3C4
(519) 727-6108
*Carries beneficial organisms
for introduction into organic
gardens, including ladybugs,
nematodes, parasitic wasps, etc.
Catalogue available.*

Nutrite
Box 160
Elmira, Ontario N3B 2Z6
(519) 669-5401 Toll-free in
Southern Ontario
1-800-265-8865
Carries organic fertilizers.

Richter's
Box 26, Goodwood
Ontario L0C 1A0
(416) 640-6677
*Carries a variety of organic
fertilizers, dormant oils,
nematodes (scan mask) for
aphids, spider mites, borers,
etc., Bt, and diatomaceous
earth. Catalogue $2.50.*

Weall and Cullen
400 Alden Road
Markham, Ontario L3R 4C1
(416) 479-0230
*Carries organic fertilizers,
aerators, traps, compost bins,
and screens.*

William Dam Seeds
Box 8400
Dundas, Ontario L9H 6M1
(416) 628-6641
*Carries organic fertilizers, pest-
resistant seeds, diatomaceous
earth, green manures, Bt, etc.
Won't ship fertilizers.*

QUEBEC
Aquaterre
155 St. Jean Baptiste
Bic, Comté de Rimouski Quebec
G0L 1B0
(418) 736-8060
Carries organic fertilizers.

Le Reveil de la Nature
R.R. 1 St-Philbert
Beauce, Quebec G0M 1X0
(418) 228-0484
*Carries organic fertilizers and
natural pest control agents.
Catalogue $1.*

Nutrite
Box 1000
Brossard, Quebec J4Z 3N2
(514) 462-2555
Carries organic fertilizers.

NEW BRUNSWICK
Hayward's Potato House
R.R. #6
Woodstock, N.B. E0J 2B0
(506) 328-3650
*Carries organic fertilizers,
diatomaceous earth, dormant
oil, traps, etc.*

Mayfield Greenhouses
R.R. #2 Gore Farm
St. Stephen, N.B. E3L 2X9
(506) 466-4230
*Carries organic fertilizers,
diatomaceous earth, dormant
oils, traps, Bt, etc.*

NOVA SCOTIA
Halifax Seed Company
P.O. Box 8026, Station A
Halifax, N.S. B3K 5L8
(902) 454-7456
*Carries diatomaceous earth,
compost bins, green manures,
pest-resistant seeds, organic
fertilizers, Bt. Free catalogue.*

Shades of Harmony
Box 598
Kingston, N.S. B0P 1R0
(902) 765-4554
*Carries seaweed-based
fertilizers, diatomaceous earth,
untreated seeds, and
insecticidal soaps. Have
landscaping business.*

PRINCE EDWARD ISLAND
Bunbury Nursery
57 Bunbury Road
Charlottetown, P.E.I. C1A 7G5
(902) 569-2207
*Carries bone meal, dormant
oils, Tanglefoot, Bt, and
insecticidal soaps.*

Island Fertilizer
19 Riverside Dr.
Charlottetown, P.E.I. C1A 7K7
(902) 566-5597
*Carries Sulpomag, bone meal,
and other natural fertilizers.*

Vesey's Seeds Ltd.
York, Charlottetown
P.E.I. C0A 1P0
(902) 892-1048
*Carries bone meal, traps,
manures, and pest-resistant
lawn seed.*

NEWFOUNDLAND AND LABRADOR

Holland Nurseries
401 Torbay Road
P.O. Box 5325
St. John's, Newfoundland
A1C 5W1
(709) 726-1283
Carries insecticidal soaps,
landscape fabric, manures,
bone meal, sticky traps, etc.

Gaze Seed Co.
9 Buchanan Street
P.O. Box 640
St. John's Newfoundland A1C 5K8
(709) 722-4590
Carries traps, insecticidal
soaps, dormant oils, pest-
resistant seeds, and some
organic fertilizers.

Soil Testing and Pest Identification Labs:

The soil testing laboratories listed below do not provide organic results unless otherwise indicated. The labs (marked ❧) provide organic results, *but only on request*. Others may exist which we have not discovered—ask your local lab. Some provincial and private labs are beginning to respond to the demand for organics: lobby your local lab to provide this service.

BRITISH COLUMBIA

Soil Testing:
Griffin Labs Corp.
1875 Spall Road
Kelowna, B.C. V1Y 4R2
(604) 861-3234

❧ Norwest Soil Research Inc:
203-20771 Langley Bypass
Langley, B.C. V3A 5E8
(604) 530-4344

ALBERTA

Soil Testing:
Alberta Soils and Animal Nutrition Lab.
905 O.S. Longman Building
6909-116 Alberts Street
Edmonton, Alberta T6H 4P2
(403) 427-2727

Pest Identification:
Alberta Environmental Centre
Plant Services Division
Bag 4000
Vegreville, Alberta T0B 4L0
(403) 632-6767
Will refer to labs in other areas.

SASKATCHEWAN

Soil Testing:
❧ Saskatchewan Soil Testing Lab
Department of Soil Science
General Purpose Building
University of Saskatchewan
Saskatoon, Saskatchewan
S7N 0W0
(306) 966-6890

Pest Identification:
Meewasin Garden Line
Department of Horticulture
University of Saskatchewan
Saskatoon, Saskatchewan
S7N 0W0
(306) 966-5855

MANITOBA

SOIL TESTING:

Manitoba Provincial Soil Testing Lab
Department of Soil Sciences
Room 262 Ellis Building
University of Manitoba
Winnipeg
Manitoba R3T 2N2
(204) 474-9257

PEST IDENTIFICATION:

Manitoba Agriculture Entomology
Section 911-401 York Ave.
Winnipeg
Manitoba R3C 0P8
(204) 945-3857

ONTARIO

SOIL TESTING:

Nutrite
Box 160
Elmira
Ontario N3B 2Z6
(519) 669-5401
Toll-free in Southern Ontario,
1-800-265-8865.

PEST IDENTIFICATION:

Pest Diagnostic Advisory Clinic
Rm B14 Graham Hall
University of Guelph
Guelph
Ontario N1G 2W1
(519) 824-4120

QUEBEC

SOIL TESTING:

Nutrite
Box 1000
Brossard
Quebec J4Z 3N2
(514) 462-2555

PEST IDENTIFICATION:

National Identification Service
Room 3119
K.W. Neatby Building
Ottawa
Ontario K1A OC6
(613) 995-5222

NEW BRUNSWICK

SOIL TESTING AND PEST IDENTIFICATION:

Plant Industry Branch
Department of Agriculture
P.O. Box 6000
Fredericton
N.B. E3B 5H1
(506) 453-2108

NOVA SCOTIA

SOIL TESTING:

Soils and Crops Branch
Nova Scotia Department of Agriculture and Marketing
P.O. Box 550, Truro
N.S. B2N 5E3
(902) 895-4469

PEST IDENTIFICATION:

ᴥ Horticulture and Biology Branch

Nova Scotia Department of Agriculture and Marketing
P.O. Box 550, Truro
N.S. B2N 5E3
(902) 895-1570

PRINCE EDWARD ISLAND

SOIL TESTING:

P.E.I Department of Agriculture

Soil and Feed Testing lab
P.O. Box 1600, Research Station
Charlottetown
P.E.I. C1A 7N3
(902) 368-5631

PEST IDENTIFICATION:

ᴥ P.E.I Dept. of Agriculture

Master Gardener Program
P.O. Box 1600, Research Station
Charlottetown
P.E.I. C1A 7N3
(902) 368-5619

NEWFOUNDLAND AND LABRADOR

SOIL TESTING:

Soil and Land Management Division

Provincial Agriculture Building
P.O. Box 4750
St John's
Newfoundland A1C 5T7
(709) 576-6738

PEST IDENTIFICATION:

Research Station

Agriculture Canada
P.O. Box 7098
St. John's
Newfoundland A1E 3Y3
(709) 772-4619

ORGANIC SOIL-TESTING LABORATORIES, USA

These labs specialize in giving organic soil test results, and some sell organic fertilizers. Write for prices and custom information if you are ordering fertilizers from Canada.

LaRamie Soils Service

P.O. Box 255
Laramie
Wyoming
USA 82070

Timberleaf Farm

5569 State Street
Albany
Ohio
USA 45710.

FURTHER READING:

Some of these will serve as reference at your local library, while others will become an invaluable part of your personal collection.

"All About Weeds." Edward Spencer, Dover Press, 1974.

"Beneficial Insects." Lester A. Swann, Harper & Row, 1964.

"Carrots Love Tomatoes." Louise Riotte, Garden Way, 1975.

"The Chemical-Free Lawn." Rodale Press, 1989.

"Ecological Pest Control: Confronting the Causes." Dr. Stuart Hill, Macdonald College, McGill University, 1983.

"The Encyclopedia of Organic Gardening." Rodale Press, 1978.

"Gardening Without Poisons." B.T. Hunter, Houghton Mifflin, 1971.

"The Harrowsmith Northern Gardener." Jennifer Bennett, Camden House, 1982.

"Insects That Feed On Trees And Shrubs." W.T. Johnson, Constock, 1976.

"The Politics Of Cancer." S. Epstein, Sierra Club Books, 1978.

"Rodale's Colour Handbook of Garden Insects", A. Carr, Rodale Press, 1978.

"The Self-Sufficient Gardener." John Seymour, Doubleday, 1980.

"The Sunset Guide To Organic Gardening", Lane Publishing, 1970.

"Sunset Pruning Handbook." Lane Publishing, 1972.

FRIENDS OF THE EARTH

One in three Canadians now considers the environment the most pressing issue in the country. We know you are concerned since you have picked up this book.

BUT WE DON'T HAVE THE LUXURY OF TIME.

The earth, our life support system, is threatened.

FRIENDS OF THE EARTH NEEDS YOUR HELP TO PROTECT THE PLANET

Friends of the Earth is the largest network of environmental groups in the world, with offices in 38 countries and half a million members worldwide. Friends of the Earth has been campaigning internationally for positive change for over 20 years.

Since 1978, Friends of the Earth Canada has been on the leading edge of environmental activism, campaigning for solutions to critical problems facing the planet today.

We have made a lasting difference with campaigns to protect the ozone layer, stop air pollution that causes global warming, ban the toxic herbicide Alachlor, teach students about tropical rainforests, ban leaded gasoline and promote energy conservation. Our new tree-planting campaign, called Global ReLeaf, gives Canadians the chance to take positive environmental action to fight global warming. Trees strategically planted in cities and towns absorb carbon dioxide, save on heating and cooling bills and filter pollution.

And since people want to know how they can participate in environmental protection, Friends of the Earth provides useful "what you can do" information. *Clean House, Clean Earth,* for example, is a guide to cleaning your house with the environment in mind.

THE 1990s: YOUR CHANCE TO ACT

Years of abuse have left their mark on the face of the earth. Many scientists fear that the earth cannot take one more decade of destruction.

The 1990s offer a window of opportunity for change. The message for us is loud and clear. Action today is crucial if we are to give our children the option of enjoying the planet tomorrow.

WHAT KEEPS US GOING?

First and foremost, your support. Contributions from individuals make our advocacy, research and education campaigns
possible. Your membership helps make our pro-environment
voice impossible to ignore.

Environmental problems are complex. But the solutions can be
as simple as changing a light-bulb or riding a bike. By joining
us, you can become part of the solution. Become part of a team
working to protect the earth for tomorrow. You can make a
difference.

Photo: Chris Staples/PhotoWorks

Carole Rubin

The author's avid interest in
organic gardening dates back to
the early 50s when we she was
discovered eating "earth-bur-
gers" in her mother's organic
flower beds in Aurora, Ontario.

Long since cured of the habit,
she has spent the past 10 years
lobbying for reform of pesticide laws and promoting organic alternatives to pesticide
use in all sectors.

Ms. Rubin is the Director of the B.C. Coalition for Alternatives
to Pesticides, and a Director of the West Coast Environmental
Law Association. She is co-chair of the pesticide caucus of the
Canadian Environmental Network and cultivates her own garden, time permitting, on the Sunshine Coast of British Colum-
bia.

I'LL HELP!

☐ I Pledge to keep my property chemical-free. Count my _____ sq.ft./sq.meters/acres/hectares IN!

☐ I'm a friend of the earth! Sign me up! Here is a tax deductible donation of $ _____ to boost the number of chemical-free acres in Canada. (The first $10 which covers membership services, is not tax creditable)

☐ A cheque for $ _____ payable to Friends of the Earth is enclosed.

☐ Charge $ _____ to my VIAS / MasterCard.

Card Number: _____

Expiry Date: _____

Signature: _____

Name: _____

Address: _____

City: _____

Province: _____ Code: _____

Telephone #: (____) _____

YOU CAN HELP YOUR ENVIRONMENT:

By reading this book and following the good gardening advice in it, you are helping to clean up your environment.

You can help even more by pledging your property "chemical-free." Friends of the Earth is counting up the chemical-free hectares of lawns and gardens in Canada to prove that people really are willing to clean up their own backyards.

Join Friends of the Earth and find out about other ways to help.

SEND TO:

Friends of the Earth
701-251 Laurier Ave. W.
Ottawa, Ontario
K1P 5J6

Christ for Real

How to Grow into God's Likeness

Books by Charles W. Price

Alive in Christ: How to Find Renewed Spiritual Power
Christ for Real: How to Grow into God's Likeness